diabetic LIVING™ holiday COOKING

VOLUME 1

DIABETIC LIVING™ HOLIDAY COOKING IS
PART OF A BOOK SERIES PUBLISHED BY
BETTER HOMES AND GARDENS SPECIAL
INTEREST MEDIA, DES MOINES, IOWA

Cranberry-Hazelnut Tarts
recipe, page 129

(holidays are magical)

When I was little, I knew the much-anticipated holidays were on the way when our grandmother started baking her buttery cookies. We all loved them and knew them by their Norwegian names. As we grew older, Grandma taught us how to bake her family recipes. I've since shared my favorites with my nieces to pass along the tradition.

Now that I've learned more about diabetes, I realize how precious those cookie-baking memories can be. It's difficult to give up the foods you've loved since childhood. The good news is that you don't have to, as you can see by the cookies on our cover and the recipes throughout this book. At *Diabetic Living*® magazine, we work hard in our Test Kitchen to create healthful yet delicious recipes that you and your family will enjoy. In this handy cookbook, you'll find our best holiday recipes from our fall and winter issues, plus some you've never seen before.

So now you can share an amazing appetizer at your coworker's holiday open house or cook a memorable holiday meal when the family gathers to celebrate. And best yet, you can savor festive holiday cookies, similar to the ones you, and I, enjoyed as children when our grandmothers rolled up their sleeves to bake. What better gift than to relive those happy days, knowing that every recipe in *Diabetic Living Holiday Cooking* is as good for you as it is tasty! Have a happy holiday, this year and every year to come!

Julia Martinusen
Julia Martinusen, Editor

ON THE COVER: Sugar Cookie Cutouts (recipe, *page 122*), Lemon Cardamom Meringue Cookies (recipe, *page 131*), *and* Raspberry-Fig Linzer Cookies (recipe, *page 121*).

Cover photograph: Robert Jacobs

diabetic LIVING holiday COOKING VOLUME 1

Editorial Director	JOHN RIHA
Creative Director	BRIDGET SANDQUIST
Editor	JULIA MARTINUSEN
Design Director	TED ROSSITER
Contributing Editor	KRISTI THOMAS, R.D.
Senior Editor	JEANNE AMBROSE
Health Editor	MADHU GADIA, R.D., CDE
Interactive Editor	RACHEL MARTIN
Contributing Copy Editor	GRETCHEN KAUFFMAN
Test Kitchen Director	LYNN BLANCHARD
Test Kitchen Product Supervisor	LAURA MARZEN, R.D.
Contributing Proofreader	PEGI BEVINS
Contributing Recipe Editors	SHARYL HEIKEN
	ROSEMARY HUTCHINSON
Administrative Assistant	MARLENE TODD
Deputy Art Director	STEPHANIE HUNTER
Contributing Designer	JILL BUDDEN
Associate Art Director	MICHELLE BILYEU
Assistant Photo Editor	RACHEL DIERENFIELD

EDITORIAL ADMINISTRATION

Managing Editor	KATHLEEN ARMENTROUT
Copy Chief	DOUG KOUMA
Office Manager	CINDY SLOBASZEWSKI
Senior Copy Editors	ELIZABETH KEEST SEDREL,
	JENNIFER SPEER RAMUNDT

EDITORIAL SERVICES

Color/Quality Manager	DALE TUNENDER
Photo Studio Manager	JEFF ANDERSON
Color/Quality Analyst	MIKE FLAHERTY
Prepress Desktop Specialist	LESLIE GARRETT

MEREDITH PUBLISHING GROUP

President JACK GRIFFIN
Executive Vice President DOUG OLSON
Editorial Director MIKE LAFAVORE
Finance and Administration MIKE RIGGS **Manufacturing** BRUCE HESTON
Consumer Marketing DAVE BALL **Corporate Sales** JACK BAMBERGER
Interactive Media LAUREN WIENER
Corporate Marketing NANCY WEBER **Research** BRITTA WARE

Meredith CORPORATION

President and Chief Executive Officer STEPHEN M. LACY
Chairman of the Board WILLIAM T. KERR
In Memoriam — E.T. MEREDITH III (1933-2003)

Diabetic Living™ *Holiday Cooking* is part of a series published by the Better Homes and Gardens Special Interest Media Group of Meredith Corp., 1716 Locust St., Des Moines, IA 50309-3023

If you have comments or questions about the editorial material in *Diabetic Living Holiday Cooking,* write to the editor of Better Homes and Gardens® *Diabetic Living*® magazine, Meredith Corp., 1716 Locust St., Des Moines, IA 50309-3023. Send an e-mail to editor@diabeticlivingonline.com or call 800/678-2651. Better Homes and Gardens *Diabetic Living* magazine is available by subscription or on the newsstand. To order a subscription to *Diabetic Living* magazine, go to www.diabeticlivingonline.com. Or write to Better Homes and Gardens *Diabetic Living* magazine, Customer Service, P.O. Box 37789, Boone, IA 50037-0789.

contents

Cranberry Poached
Pears, recipe, page 140

holiday party appetizers

White Bean and Tomato Bruschetta

Gather with friends at a *holiday open house* or a casual after-work get-together to share your best *wishes for the season.* The evening turns cozy when you offer *tantalizing* trays of appetizers, such as bruschetta—topped with holiday red and green—or cheesy stuffed mushrooms and *delightful* cracker spreads. When you pour the bubbly, *you'll be the hit* of your party.

White Bean and Tomato Bruschetta

The topper tastes creamy, yet the beans have very little fat.

PER APPETIZER: 75 cal., 2 g total fat (0 g sat. fat), 0 mg chol., 184 mg sodium, 11 g carb., 1 g fiber, 3 g pro. Exchanges: 1 starch. Carb choices: 1.

- 2 tablespoons oil-packed dried tomatoes
- ½ cup snipped fresh watercress or fresh flat-leaf parsley
- 2 tablespoons pine nuts, toasted
- 1 cup canned white kidney beans (cannellini beans), rinsed and drained
- 1 tablespoon fat-free milk
- 2 to 3 teaspoons lemon juice
- 1 teaspoon snipped fresh thyme or ¼ teaspoon dried thyme, crushed
- ¼ teaspoon salt
- ¼ teaspoon ground black pepper
- 2 cloves garlic, cut up
- 12 ½-inch-thick slices baguette-style French bread
  Watercress sprigs (optional)

1. Preheat broiler. Drain the tomatoes, reserving oil; finely snip. In a small bowl, combine tomatoes, 1 teaspoon reserved oil, ½ cup watercress, and nuts; set aside.

2. In a food processor or blender, combine 1 teaspoon reserved oil, the beans, milk, lemon juice, thyme, salt, pepper, and garlic. Cover and process until smooth; set bean mixture aside.

3. On an ungreased baking sheet, arrange bread slices. Broil 4 inches from heat for 1½ to 2 minutes or until lightly toasted, turning once.

4. Spread about 1 tablespoon bean mixture onto each slice, spreading to edges. Broil 4 inches from heat about 1 minute or until bean mixture is warm. Top each with tomato mixture. If desired, garnish with watercress sprigs. Serve warm. Makes 12 appetizers.

Herbed Peppers and Olives

Mix and match olive colors, sizes, and shapes.

PER SERVING: 89 cal., 7 g total fat (1 g sat. fat), 0 mg chol., 355 mg sodium, 6 g carb., 2 g fiber, 0 g pro. Exchanges: 0.5 vegetable, 1.5 fat. Carb choices: 0.5.

- 2 teaspoons olive oil
- 2 cloves garlic, minced
- 2 medium red sweet peppers, seeded and cut into thin strips
- 1 medium banana pepper, seeded and sliced thinly
- 12 ounces assorted unpitted olives (about 2 cups)
- 2 teaspoons snipped fresh oregano or ½ teaspoon dried oregano, crushed

1. In a large skillet, heat oil over medium heat. Add garlic; cook and stir for 30 seconds. Add peppers; cook and stir about 4 minutes or until tender.

2. Add the olives and oregano; cook and stir for 2 minutes or until warm. Serve olive mixture warm. Makes 12 (¼-cup) servings.

Tomato and Basil Chèvre Spread

Soak dried tomatoes in water instead of using the oil-packed kind. Serve spread with crackers.

PER 2 TABLESPOONS: 66 cal., 5 g total fat (3 g sat. fat), 14 mg chol., 125 mg sodium, 2 g carb., 0 g fiber, 4 g pro. Exchanges: 0.5 high-fat meat. Carb choices: 0.

- ⅓ cup dried tomatoes (not oil-packed)
- 4 ounces soft goat cheese (chèvre)
- ½ of an 8-ounce package reduced-fat cream cheese (Neufchâtel), softened
- ¼ cup snipped fresh basil or 2 teaspoons dried basil, crushed
- 3 cloves garlic, minced
- ⅛ teaspoon ground black pepper
- 1 to 2 tablespoons fat-free milk

1. In a bowl, cover tomatoes with boiling water; let stand for 10 minutes. Drain; snip tomatoes.

2. Stir in goat cheese, cream cheese, basil, garlic, and pepper. Stir in enough milk to make a spreading consistency. Cover and chill for 2 to 4 hours. Makes about 1¼ cups spread or 10 (2-tablespoon) servings.

Tomato and Basil
Chèvre Spread

Pesto and Tomato Bruschetta

Arugula adds a twist to the traditional Italian pine nut pesto.

PER SERVING: 89 cal., 3 g total fat (1 g sat. fat), 3 mg chol., 246 mg sodium, 11 g carb., 1 g fiber, 4 g pro. Exchanges: 1 starch, 0.5 fat. Carb choices: 1.

- 1 recipe Pine Nut Pesto (see below)
- 24 ½-inch-thick slices baguette-style French bread, toasted, or whole grain crackers
- 1 ounce Parmesan or Romano cheese, shaved
- 1 cup red and/or yellow cherry tomatoes, halved or quartered, or 2 plum tomatoes, sliced
  Fresh basil sprigs (optional)
  Pine nuts, chopped walnuts, or chopped almonds, toasted (optional)

1. Spread Pine Nut Pesto onto baguette slices. Top with Parmesan and tomatoes. If desired, top with basil and nuts. Makes 12 (2-slice) servings.

Pine Nut Pesto: In a small food processor, combine 1 cup firmly packed fresh basil; 1 cup torn fresh arugula or spinach; ¼ cup grated Parmesan or Romano cheese; ¼ cup toasted pine nuts, chopped walnuts, or chopped almonds; 1 quartered clove garlic; 1 tablespoon olive oil; 1 tablespoon white balsamic vinegar; and ¼ teaspoon salt. Cover and process with several on/off turns until a paste forms, stopping several times to scrape the side. Process in enough water, adding 1 tablespoon at a time, until pesto reaches the consistency of soft butter.

Make-Ahead Directions: Toast bread slices and prepare Pine Nut Pesto as directed. Cover and chill for up to 24 hours. Serve as directed in Step 1.

(top it off)

Whether you call them bruschetta or crostini, toasted slices of French bread make a sturdy base for many spreads and toppers. You can also use toasted pita triangles, thinly sliced party breads, or multigrain crackers for the same types of toppers. And if you're concerned about too many carbohydrates, bias-slice fresh zucchini or cucumber for a colorful and crunchy base.

Herbed Peppers and Olives

Jamaican Jerk Shrimp with Papaya and Pineapple

Wintertime guests will delight in this sunny Carribean-style appetizer. Serve it in a chilled clear-glass bowl on the buffet or in individual portions in chilled martini glasses.

PER SERVING: 107 cal., 2 g total fat (0 g sat. fat), 148 mg chol., 246 mg sodium, 6 g carb., 1 g fiber, 16 g pro. Exchanges: 2 very lean meat, 0.5 fruit. Carb choices: 0.5

2 **pounds fresh or frozen peeled, cooked large shrimp (with tails)**
1 **tablespoon Jamaican jerk seasoning***
1 **tablespoon cooking oil**
½ **of a 24- to 26-ounce jar refrigerated sliced papaya, drained and coarsely chopped (1¼ cups)**
1 **8-ounce can pineapple tidbits, drained and chopped**
¼ **cup chopped roasted red sweet peppers**
¼ **cup sliced green onions**
1 **teaspoon finely shredded lime peel**
2 **tablespoons lime juice**
2 **cloves garlic, minced**
   Green onions (optional)

1. Thaw shrimp, if frozen. Place shrimp in a resealable plastic bag. Add jerk seasoning and oil to shrimp. Seal bag; turn to coat shrimp. Chill for 30 minutes.

2. Meanwhile, in a medium bowl, combine papaya, pineapple, sweet peppers, sliced green onions, lime peel, lime juice, and garlic. Cover and chill papaya mixture until serving time.

3. To serve, gently stir together shrimp and fruit mixture. If desired, garnish with whole green onions. Makes 12 (½-cup) servings.

*Test Kitchen Tip: Look for jerk seasoning in the herb and spice section of a large supermarket. To make homemade jerk seasoning, in a small bowl, combine 1½ teaspoons dried thyme, ½ teaspoon ground allspice, ½ teaspoon ground black pepper, ⅛ teaspoon salt, ⅛ teaspoon ground cinnamon, and ⅛ teaspoon cayenne pepper. Store in an airtight container or screw-top jar for several months in a cool dark place.

Shrimp with Basil

Shrimp Spring Rolls

Look for fish sauce in Asian markets or
use reduced-sodium soy sauce.

PER ROLL: 65 cal., 0 g total fat (0 g sat. fat), 10 mg chol., 55 mg sodium,
13 g carb., 1 g fiber, 2 g pro. Exchanges: 0.5 starch, 0.5 carb. Carb choices: 1.

- **2** ounces dried rice vermicelli noodles
- **24** medium shrimp, peeled and deveined
- **2** cups shredded Chinese cabbage
- **1** cup shredded carrots
- **½** cup fresh cilantro
- **½** cup fresh mint or flat-leaf parsley
- **24** 8½-inch round rice papers
- **1** recipe Rice Vinegar Dipping Sauce (see below)

1. In a medium saucepan, cook noodles in lightly salted boiling water for 3 minutes; drain. Rinse under cold water; drain well. Use kitchen shears to snip noodles into small pieces; set aside.

2. In a large saucepan, cook shrimp in lightly salted boiling water for 1 to 2 minutes or until pink; drain. Rinse with cold water; drain again. Halve shrimp lengthwise; set aside.

3. For filling, in a large bowl, stir together cooked vermicelli, shredded cabbage, shredded carrots, cilantro, and mint; set aside.

4. Pour warm water into a shallow dish. Dip rice papers, one at a time, into water; gently shake off excess. Place rice papers between clean, damp, 100-percent-cotton kitchen towels; let stand for 10 minutes.

5. To assemble, brush edges of a rice paper round with a little warm water (keep others covered). Place a well-rounded tablespoon of filling across lower third of softened rice paper. Fold bottom of rice paper over filling; arrange 2 shrimp halves across filling. Fold in paper sides. Tightly roll up paper and filling. Place, seam side down, on a platter. Repeat with remaining rice paper, filling, and shrimp. Cover and chill until ready to serve. Serve with Rice Vinegar Dipping Sauce. Makes 24 spring rolls.

Rice Vinegar Dipping Sauce: In a small saucepan, combine ½ cup water and 2 tablespoons sugar. Bring to boiling over medium heat until sugar is dissolved, stirring occasionally. Remove from heat; stir in 2 tablespoons rice wine vinegar, 1 tablespoon fish sauce or reduced-sodium soy sauce, and 1 tablespoon finely shredded carrot.

Make-Ahead Directions: Prepare as directed through Step 5. Cover with a damp cloth; chill for up to 6 hours. Prepare dipping sauce; cover and chill for up to 24 hours.

Shrimp with Basil

Fresh basil and balsamic vinegar add flavor
to classic scampi.

PER APPETIZER: 52 cal., 2 g total fat (1 g sat. fat), 53 mg chol.,
95 mg sodium, 1 g carb., 0 g fiber, 7 g pro. Exchanges: 1 very lean meat,
0.5 fat. Carb choices: 0.

- **16** fresh or frozen large shrimp in shells (about 12 ounces)
- **3** to 4 cloves garlic, minced
- **1** tablespoon butter
- **¼** cup snipped fresh basil
- **1** tablespoon white balsamic vinegar
- **⅛** teaspoon salt
- **Fresh watercress or parsley (optional)**

1. Thaw shrimp, if frozen. Rinse shrimp; pat dry with paper towels.

2. Preheat broiler. Use a sharp knife to split each shrimp down the back through shell almost all the way through the meaty portion, leaving tails intact, if desired. Devein shrimp. Loosen shell or remove shrimp from shell. Flatten shrimp with your hand or the flat side of knife blade. On the unheated rack of a broiler pan, arrange shrimp, split sides up, in a single layer.

3. Meanwhile, in a small saucepan, cook garlic in hot butter until tender. Stir in basil, white balsamic vinegar, and salt.

4. Brush shrimp with garlic mixture. Broil 3 to 4 inches from heat for 5 to 8 minutes or just until shrimp are pink. Serve warm. Transfer shrimp to a platter. If desired, garnish with watercress. Makes 8 (2-shrimp) appetizers.

Make-Ahead Directions: Prepare as directed through Step 2. Cover and chill for up to 6 hours. Continue as directed in Steps 3 and 4.

Ginger Shrimp Skewers

These colorful skewers will beautify your party buffet. Ginger, orange, and sesame combine for a zesty Pacific Rim marinade.

PER KABOB: 44 cal., 1 g total fat (0 g sat. fat), 48 mg chol., 58 mg sodium, 2 g carb., 0 g fiber, 7 g pro. Exchanges: 1 very lean meat. Carb choices: 0.

- 16 fresh or frozen large shrimp in shells (about 12 ounces)
- 1 teaspoon finely shredded orange peel
- 3 tablespoons orange juice
- 1 tablespoon white wine vinegar
- 1 teaspoon toasted sesame oil or olive oil
- 1 teaspoon grated fresh ginger or ½ teaspoon ground ginger
- ⅛ teaspoon salt
- ⅛ teaspoon cayenne pepper
- 1 clove garlic, minced
- 16 fresh pea pods
- 8 canned mandarin orange sections
  Reduced-sodium soy sauce (optional)

1. Thaw shrimp, if frozen. Peel and devein, leaving tails intact (if desired). In a large saucepan, cook shrimp in boiling water for 1 to 3 minutes or until pink; drain. Rinse with cold water; drain. Place in a resealable plastic bag set in a bowl.

2. For marinade, in a small bowl, combine orange peel, orange juice, vinegar, oil, ginger, salt, cayenne pepper, and garlic; pour mixture over shrimp. Seal bag; turn to coat. Marinate in the refrigerator for 1 to 2 hours, turning bag occasionally.

3. Place pea pods in a steamer basket over boiling water. Cover; steam for 2 to 3 minutes or until tender. Rinse with cold water; drain.

4. Drain shrimp, discarding marinade. Wrap a pea pod around each shrimp. On each of eight 6-inch skewers, thread 2 shrimp and 1 orange section. If desired, serve with reduced-sodium soy sauce. Makes 8 kabobs.

Ginger Shrimp Skewers

Caper Shrimp Phyllo Tarts

Miniature phyllo shells and sour cream dip mean these extraordinary tarts are easy and great tasting.

PER TART: 51 cal., 2 g total fat (0 g sat. fat), 32 mg chol., 106 mg sodium, 3 g carb., 0 g fiber, 4 g pro. Exchanges: 1 lean meat. Carb choices: 0.

- ¾ cup dairy sour cream dill dip
- ½ teaspoon finely shredded lemon peel
- 1 teaspoon lemon juice
- 2 2.1-ounce packages baked miniature phyllo dough shells (30 total)
- 2 tablespoons capers, drained
- 30 small to medium shrimp (tails intact, if desired), peeled, deveined, and cooked
  Fresh dill sprigs (optional)
  Finely shredded lemon peel (optional)

1. In a small bowl, stir together dill dip, the ½ teaspoon lemon peel, and the lemon juice. Fill phyllo shells with dill dip mixture (about 1 teaspoon per shell). Sprinkle with capers. In each shell, place 1 shrimp with tail up. If desired, garnish with dill sprigs and additional finely shredded lemon peel. Makes 30 tarts.

Make-Ahead Directions: Prepare as directed. Cover and chill for up to 2 hours.

Pistachio Salmon Nuggets

A sprinkling of pistachios adds even more
heart-healthy benefits.

PER SERVING: 74 cal., 4 g total fat (1 g sat. fat), 24 mg chol., 88 mg sodium,
0 g carb., 0 g fiber, 9 g pro. Exchanges: 1 lean meat, 0.5 fat. Carb
choices: 0.

- 1 pound fresh or frozen skinless salmon fillets, about
     1 inch thick
- 2 tablespoons water
- 2 tablespoons reduced-sodium soy sauce
- 1 tablespoon grated fresh ginger
- 2 teaspoons toasted sesame oil or cooking oil
- 1 tablespoon cooking oil
- 1 tablespoon finely chopped pistachio nuts

1. Thaw fish, if frozen. Rinse fish; pat dry with paper
towels. Cut fish into 1-inch chunks. Place fish in a
resealable plastic bag set in a shallow dish.

2. For marinade, in a small bowl, combine the water,
soy sauce, ginger, and the 2 teaspoons sesame oil. Pour
marinade onto salmon chunks in bag. Seal bag; turn to
coat salmon. Marinate in the refrigerator for 30 minutes,
turning bag occasionally.

Quick Tip:

The best appetizers are
those that need zero time
in the kitchen right before
or during your party. That
means getting a head start.
Marinating and stirring up
dips are no-brainers, but
why not shape meatballs,
thread kabobs, or
precook vegetables
or eggs ahead?

3. Drain salmon, discarding marinade. In a large
nonstick skillet, heat the 1 tablespoon cooking oil over
medium-high heat. Add half of the salmon chunks to
skillet; cook and gently stir for 3 to 5 minutes or until
fish flakes easily with a fork. Remove from skillet and
place on paper towels. Cook and stir remaining fish;
remove and place on paper towels. Transfer to a platter;
sprinkle with pistachio nuts. Makes 10 to
12 appetizer servings.

Pistachio Salmon Nuggets

Lamb Meat Balls
with Cucumber Raita

Tandoori Chicken Wings

Add a taste of the exotic to your appetizer buffet with this take on a classic Indian chicken dish known for its red color and tantalizing flavor. These spicy wings bake in your oven, not a tandoor, and your guests will love them.

PER SERVING: 119 cal., 4 g total fat (1 g sat. fat), 62 mg chol., 363 mg sodium, 3 g carb., 0 g fiber, 16 g pro. Exchanges: 2 lean meat. Carb choices: 0.

- 5 pounds chicken drumettes* (about 50 drumettes)
- 1 medium onion, cut into wedges
- 1 8-ounce can tomato sauce
- 1 6-ounce carton plain fat-free yogurt
- 1 tablespoon ground coriander
- 4 cloves garlic, coarsely chopped
- 2 teaspoons chopped fresh ginger
- 1½ teaspoons salt
- 1 teaspoon cumin seeds
- 1 teaspoon garam masala
- ½ to 1 teaspoon cayenne pepper (optional)
- ¼ to ½ teaspoon red food coloring
- 2 whole cloves
  Lemon wedges (optional)
  Thin wedges red onion (optional)

1. Place the chicken drumettes in a 3-quart rectangular baking dish; set aside.
2. For the tandoori masala, in a blender or food processor, combine onion, tomato sauce, yogurt, coriander, garlic, ginger, salt, cumin seeds, garam masala, cayenne pepper (if desired), red food coloring, and whole cloves. Blend to a very smooth paste. (The color should be deep red.)
3. Pour the tandoori masala over the chicken drumettes; turn chicken drumettes to coat. Cover and marinate in the refrigerator for 4 to 24 hours.
4. Preheat oven to 400°F. Arrange as many of the chicken drumettes on the unheated rack of a broiler pan as will fit in a single layer. Bake for 25 minutes. Turn oven to broil. Broil chicken 4 to 5 inches from the heat for 6 to 8 minutes or until chicken is no longer pink and pieces just start to blacken, turning drumettes once halfway through broiling.
5. Transfer drumettes to a platter. Repeat baking and broiling the remaining chicken. If desired, serve with lemon and red onion wedges. Makes 16 servings (about 3 drumettes each).

*Test Kitchen Tip: If you cannot find chicken drumettes, use 25 chicken wings instead. Cut off and discard tips of chicken wings. Cut wings at joints to form 50 pieces.

Lamb Meat Balls with Cucumber Raita

A cool and creamy cucumber sauce tames the spices.

PER MEATBALL (WITH RAITA): 68 cal., 4 g total fat (2 g sat. fat), 20 mg chol., 154 mg sodium, 2 g carb., 0 g fiber, 6 g pro. Exchanges: 1 lean meat. Carb choices: 0.

- 1 medium onion, finely chopped
- 1¼ teaspoons grated fresh ginger
- 2 or 3 cloves garlic, minced
- 1 teaspoon salt
- 1 teaspoon ground coriander
- 1 teaspoon ground cumin
- ½ teaspoon garam masala
- ¼ to ½ teaspoon cayenne pepper (optional)
- 2 pounds ground lean lamb
- 1 recipe Cucumber Raita (see below)

1. Preheat oven to 350°F. In a bowl, combine onion, ginger, garlic, salt, coriander, cumin, garam masala, and, if desired, cayenne pepper. Add lamb; mix well. Shape into 32 meatballs; place in a 15×10×1-inch baking pan.
2. Bake about 25 minutes or until cooked through. Drain off fat. Transfer meatballs to a platter. Serve with Cucumber Raita. Makes 32 meatballs.

Cucumber Raita: Peel and shred 1 medium cucumber. Place in a strainer; let stand for 15 minutes. Discard liquid. Place cucumber in a bowl; stir in one 16-ounce carton plain yogurt, 1 teaspoon Roasted Cumin Powder (see below), ¾ teaspoon salt, and, if desired, ¼ teaspoon cayenne pepper. Cover and chill until serving time.

Roasted Cumin Powder: In a small dry skillet in a well-ventilated area, heat 1 tablespoon cumin seeds over medium heat for 5 to 6 minutes or until smoke begins to rise and seeds begin to brown. Remove from skillet. Cool. Grind seeds with a mortar and pestle or a spice grinder.

(stuff it!)

Mushrooms, miniature sweet peppers, cherry tomatoes, and hard-cooked eggs all make great mini cups for flavorful fillings. And mini means bite-size portions, so you can eat more reasonably, too. To help control how much filling you use, fill a pastry bag with a large star tip to pipe the filling into your mini cups. If you don't have a pastry bag, simply spoon the filling into a resealable plastic bag, twist to close, cut off a bottom corner, and squeeze just the right amount of filling into your mini cups. They're not only delicious, they look pretty, too!

Herbed Cheese
Mini Peppers

Herbed Cheese Mini Peppers
You can substitute sweet pepper wedges
for the mini peppers.

PER APPETIZER: 32 cal., 3 g total fat (2 g sat. fat), 9 mg chol., 46 mg sodium, 1 g carb., 0 g fiber, 1 g pro. Exchanges: 0.5 fat. Carb choices: 0.

- **10** red, yellow, and/or orange miniature sweet peppers (6 to 8 ounces total)
- **1** 8-ounce package reduced-fat cream cheese (Neufchâtel), softened
- **2** tablespoons snipped fresh oregano, rosemary, tarragon, or thyme, or ½ to 1 teaspoon dried oregano, rosemary, tarragon, or thyme, crushed
- **1** tablespoon lemon juice
- **1** tablespoon fat-free milk
  Finely shredded lemon peel
  Fresh oregano leaves (optional)

1. Halve sweet peppers lengthwise; discard seeds. Set peppers aside.

2. For filling, in a small bowl, stir together cream cheese, desired herb, lemon juice, and milk. Stir in additional milk, if necessary, to make a piping consistency.

3. Pipe or spoon filling into pepper halves. Top with lemon peel. If desired, garnish with oregano leaves. Makes 20 appetizers.

Make-Ahead Directions: Prepare as directed. Cover and chill for up to 4 hours.

Four-Cheese Stuffed Mushrooms

Teaming light ricotta cheese with richer Monterey Jack, Parmesan, and feta keeps the flavor but holds down the fat.

PER MUSHROOM: 42 cal., 3 g total fat (1 g sat. fat), 8 mg chol., 105 mg sodium, 2 g carb., 0 g fiber, 3 g pro. Exchanges: 0.5 medium-fat meat. Carb choices: 0.

24 large fresh mushrooms (1½ to 2 inches in diameter)
1 tablespoon olive oil
8 dried tomatoes (not oil-packed)
1 cup light ricotta cheese
½ cup finely chopped fresh spinach
½ cup shredded Monterey Jack cheese (2 ounces)
3 tablespoons grated Parmesan cheese
1 tablespoon snipped fresh basil or 1 teaspoon dried basil, crushed
2 cloves garlic, minced
¼ teaspoon salt
¼ teaspoon ground black pepper
½ cup crumbled feta cheese (2 ounces)
Fresh basil leaves (optional)

1. Preheat oven to 350°F. Remove and discard mushroom stems. Brush caps with oil. In a shallow baking pan, arrange caps, stem sides down. Bake for 12 minutes.

2. Meanwhile, in a medium bowl, cover dried tomatoes with boiling water; let stand for 10 minutes.

3. Increase oven temperature to 450°F. Drain mushroom caps and tomatoes, discarding liquid; set mushroom caps aside.

4. For filling, in the same bowl, coarsely snip tomatoes. Stir in ricotta, spinach, Monterey Jack cheese, Parmesan cheese, snipped basil, garlic, salt, and pepper.

5. Turn mushroom caps stem sides up; fill caps with cheese filling. Sprinkle with feta cheese.

6. Bake caps for 8 to 10 minutes or until filling is heated through and light brown. Serve warm. If desired, garnish with basil leaves. Makes 24 mushrooms.

Make-Ahead Directions: Prepare as directed through Step 5. Cover and chill stuffed mushrooms for up to 24 hours. Bake as directed.

Four-Cheese Stuffed Mushrooms

Creamy Fruit Morsels

Use whichever fruit is in season for these colorful fruit bites.

PER MORSEL: 17 cal., 0 g total fat (0 g sat. fat), 1 mg chol., 39 mg sodium, 2 g carb., 0 g fiber, 1 g pro. Exchanges: Free. Carb choices: 0.

- ½ of an 8-ounce package fat-free cream cheese, softened
- ¼ cup low-sugar orange marmalade
- ¼ teaspoon almond extract
- 16 small pieces fresh fruit (such as large strawberries or large dark sweet cherries; small kiwifruits or fresh figs, peeled; and/or halved apricots)

1. In a medium bowl, beat cream cheese with an electric mixer on medium speed until fluffy; beat in orange marmalade and almond extract. If desired, place cream cheese mixture in a pastry bag fitted with a large star tip.

2. If using strawberries, figs, or cherries, slice off a small portion of the stem ends; set aside. If using cherries or apricots, pit them. Pipe or spoon cream cheese mixture on top of fruit. If using strawberries, figs, or cherries, replace stem ends of fruit.

3. Serve immediately or cover and chill for up to 1 hour before serving. Makes 16 morsels.

*Test Kitchen Tip: If necessary, cut small slices from rounded sides of fruit halves so they don't roll on the platter.

Quick Tip:

To keep party foods hot, arrange them on baking sheets ahead of time and keep them chilled until needed. Bake and serve one sheet at a time as you need it. You can also set hot appetizers on a warming tray. Or keep hot dips, meatballs, and wings warm in your slow cooker set on low.

Roasted Pepper Roll-Ups

Red and green in the filling add splashes of holiday color.

PER SERVING: 74 cal., 3 g total fat (2 g sat. fat), 6 mg chol., 165 mg sodium, 9 g carb., 1 g fiber, 3 g pro. Exchanges: 0.5 starch, 0.5 fat. Carb choices: 0.5.

- ½ of an 8-ounce package reduced-fat cream cheese (Neufchâtel), softened
- 4 ounces soft goat cheese (chèvre)
- 1 tablespoon fat-free milk
- 1 small clove garlic, minced
- ¼ teaspoon ground black pepper
- ½ cup roasted red sweet peppers, drained and finely chopped
- ¼ cup snipped fresh basil
- 8 8-inch whole wheat or plain flour tortillas
- 2 cups packed fresh spinach leaves

1. For filling, in a small mixer bowl, beat cream cheese with an electric mixer on medium speed for 30 seconds. Add goat cheese, milk, garlic, and black pepper; beat until smooth. Stir in sweet peppers and basil.

2. To assemble, divide filling among tortillas, spreading to within ½ inch of edges. Arrange spinach on filling. Roll up tightly. Cover and chill until serving time.

3. To serve, slice roll-ups into 48 (1¼-inch-wide) pieces. Makes 24 (2-slice) servings.

Make-Ahead Directions: Prepare roll-ups as directed through Step 2. Cover; chill for up to 24 hours.

Walnut-Feta Yogurt Dip

Baby carrots, cherry tomatoes, radishes, cucumber or zucchini strips, and sweet pepper strips are all terrific choices for dunking into this Mediterranean-style dip.

PER 2 TABLESPOONS: 68 cal., 4 g total fat (1 g sat. fat), 8 mg chol., 140 mg sodium, 5 g carb., 0 g fiber, 4 g pro. Exchanges: 0.5 milk, 0.5 fat. Carb choices: 0.

- 4 cups plain low-fat or fat-free yogurt*
- ½ cup crumbled feta cheese (2 ounces)
- ⅓ cup chopped walnuts or pine nuts, toasted
- 2 tablespoons snipped dried tomatoes (not oil-packed)
- 2 teaspoons snipped fresh oregano or marjoram or 1 teaspoon dried oregano or marjoram, crushed
- ¼ teaspoon salt
- ⅛ teaspoon ground black pepper
  Walnut half (optional)

1. For yogurt cheese, line a yogurt strainer, sieve, or small colander with 3 layers of 100-percent-cotton cheesecloth or a clean paper coffee filter. Suspend lined strainer over a bowl. Spoon yogurt into strainer. Cover with plastic wrap. Chill for 24 to 48 hours. Remove from refrigerator. Discard liquid in bowl.

2. Transfer yogurt cheese to a medium bowl. Stir in feta cheese, the nuts, dried tomatoes, oregano, salt, and pepper. Cover and chill for 1 to 24 hours. If desired, garnish with walnut half. Makes 2 cups or 16 (2-tablespoon) servings.

*Note: Use yogurt that contains no gums, gelatin, or fillers. These ingredients may prevent the curd and whey from separating to make the yogurt cheese.

White Bean and Pine Nut Dip

Serve dip with vegetable dippers or Toasted Pita Chips (see above right).

PER 2 TABLESPOONS: 111 cal., 2 g total fat (0 g sat. fat), 0 mg chol., 197 mg sodium, 20 g carb., 2 g fiber, 5 g pro. Exchanges: 1.5 starch. Carb choices: 1.5.

- ¼ cup soft whole wheat bread crumbs
- 2 tablespoons fat-free milk
- 1 15-ounce can white kidney (cannellini) beans or Great Northern beans, rinsed and drained
- ¼ cup fat-free dairy sour cream
- 3 tablespoons pine nuts, toasted
- ¼ teaspoon salt-free garlic-and-herb seasoning blend or other salt-free seasoning blend

- ⅛ teaspoon cayenne pepper
- 2 teaspoons snipped fresh oregano or basil or ½ teaspoon dried oregano or basil, crushed
  Fresh oregano (optional)

1. In a small bowl, combine bread crumbs and milk. Cover and let stand for 5 minutes.

2. Meanwhile, in a blender or food processor, combine beans, sour cream, pine nuts, seasoning blend, and cayenne pepper. Cover and blend or process until nearly smooth. Add bread crumb mixture. Cover and blend or process until smooth. Stir in oregano. Cover and chill for 2 to 24 hours to blend flavors.

3. If desired, garnish with oregano. Makes 1½ cups or 12 (2-tablespoon) servings.

Toasted Pita Chips: Preheat oven to 350°F. Split 4 large pita bread rounds in half horizontally. Using a sharp knife, cut each pita half into 6 wedges. Arrange wedges in a single layer on ungreased baking sheets. Coat pita wedges with nonstick cooking spray. Sprinkle lightly with paprika. Bake for 12 to 15 minutes or until wedges are crisp and golden brown. Makes 48 chips.

Tangy Lemon-Caper Dip

Serve with vegetable dippers or chilled cooled shrimp.

PER 2 TABLESPOONS: 32 cal., 2 g total fat (2 g sat. fat), 8 mg chol., 36 mg sodium, 2 g carb., 0 g fiber, 1 g pro. Exchanges: 0.5 fat. Carb choices: 0.

- 1 8-ounce carton light dairy sour cream
- ½ cup plain low-fat yogurt
- 1 tablespoon drained capers, finely chopped
- 2 teaspoons snipped fresh dill or thyme or ½ teaspoon dried dill weed or dried thyme, crushed
- ½ teaspoon finely shredded lemon peel
  Finely shredded lemon peel (optional)
  Snipped fresh dill (optional)

1. In a bowl, stir together sour cream, yogurt, capers, herb, and lemon peel. Cover; chill until serving time.

2. Before serving, stir dip. If desired, garnish with additional lemon peel and fresh dill. Serve with cut-up vegetables. Makes 1½ cups or 12 (2-tablespoon) servings.

Make-Ahead Directions: Prepare dip as directed through Step 1. Cover and chill for up to 24 hours.

(10 ways to lighten)

Lighten your party foods and menus with these tips.

1. **Question** whether you need the salt. Try none and sprinkle it on only if you need it.
2. **Add flavor** with fresh herbs and spices rather than high-sodium bottled condiments.
3. **Halve** the amount of pasta or potatoes in a recipe. You can often substitute nonstarchy vegetables for some of the pasta or potatoes.
4. **Try one crust** instead of two for sweet or savory pies. Or arrange pastry cutouts on top rather than covering the entire surface with a crust.
5. **Switch to low-fat** or fat-free dairy products, such as sour cream, yogurt, milk, and evaporated milk.
6. **Rely** on egg whites or refrigerated egg substitute instead of using whole eggs.
7. **Opt** for low-sodium or no-salt-added canned items, such as broth and tomato products.
8. **Choose** very lean beef or pork, poultry breast meat without skin, or fish.
9. **Serve** brown rice rather than white rice, whole wheat pasta rather than plain noodles, and whole wheat or corn tortillas rather than flour tortillas.
10. **Use less** cheese overall and opt for reduced-fat cheese varieties.

Walnut Feta Yogurt Dip (top),
White Bean and Pine
Nut Dip (bottom)

Quick Tip:

When you're asked to bring an appetizer to a friend's party, these colorful spirals come to the rescue. Just roll these pinwheels up to a day ahead and carry them to your party in an insulated cooler along with some ice. Dips and spreads can easily ride along, too.

Olive-Pepper Spirals

Olive-Pepper Spirals

The olive-and-caper spread is a takeoff on a classic French condiment, tapenade.

PER SLICE: 68 cal., 4 g total fat (2 g sat. fat), 5 mg chol., 137 mg sodium, 7 g carb., 1 g fiber, 1 g pro. Exchanges: 0.5 starch, 0.5 fat. Carb choices: 0.5.

- 1 cup pitted ripe or Greek olives, drained
- 1 tablespoon olive oil or cooking oil
- 2 teaspoons capers, drained
- 2 teaspoons lemon juice or lime juice
- 3 9- to 10-inch whole wheat flour tortillas (any flavor)
- ½ of an 8-ounce tub cream cheese with chive and onion
  Lettuce leaves
- 1 cup purchased roasted red sweet peppers, well drained and cut into thin strips
  Fresh flat-leaf parsley sprigs (optional)

1. In a food processor, combine olives, oil, capers, and lemon juice. Cover and process with several on/off turns until olives are very finely chopped.

2. Arrange tortillas on a flat surface. Spread one-third of the cream cheese onto each tortilla; spread one-third of the olive mixture onto each. Place several lettuce leaves on top of olive mixture. Arrange one-third of the pepper strips over lettuce on each tortilla. Roll up tortillas; wrap in plastic wrap. Chill for 1 to 4 hours.

3. To serve, slice each tortilla roll into 7 slices. Arrange spirals on a platter. If desired, garnish with parsley. Makes 21 appetizers.

Turkey-Mango Pinwheels

These turkey-and-tortilla wraps slice into festive bite-size rounds for holiday nibbling.

PER 2-SLICE SERVING: 104 cal., 3 g total fat (2 g sat. fat), 11 mg chol., 242 mg sodium, 13 g carb., 0 g fiber, 6 g pro. Exchanges: 0.5 very lean meat, 1 starch. Carb choices: 1.

- 6 ounces soft goat cheese (chèvre)
- ⅓ cup bottled mango chutney
- 4 9- to 10-inch whole wheat flour tortillas
- 8 ounces thinly sliced smoked turkey breast
- 2 cups fresh arugula or fresh spinach leaves
- 8 refrigerated mango slices, drained and patted dry

1. In a bowl, stir together goat cheese and mango chutney. Spread goat cheese mixture onto tortillas, leaving a 1-inch space along one edge of each tortilla.

2. Arrange turkey slices on goat cheese mixture. Top with arugula. Cut large mango slices in half lengthwise; place on greens opposite the 1-inch space. Roll up tortillas tightly, starting with the mango. Cover and chill for 30 minutes to 4 hours.

3. To serve, cut diagonally into ¾-inch-thick slices. Makes about 32 slices (16 servings).

Vegetable Pita Pizzas

What could be easier than pita bread as a base for pizza? Use any veggie toppers you like for these mini wedges.

PER SERVING: 113 cal., 2 g total fat (1 g sat. fat), 4 mg chol., 291 mg sodium, 20 g carb., 3 g fiber, 5 g pro. Exchanges: 1 starch, 0.5 vegetable, 0.5 fat. Carb choices: 1

- 2 large whole wheat pita bread rounds
  Nonstick cooking spray
- ½ cup assorted fresh vegetables (such as small broccoli or cauliflower florets, red sweet pepper strips, sliced fresh mushrooms, and/or chopped carrot)
- ¼ cup pizza sauce
- ¼ cup shredded mozzarella cheese (1 ounce)

1. Preheat oven to 400°F. Place pita bread rounds on a baking sheet. Bake for 5 minutes.

2. Meanwhile, coat an unheated small skillet with nonstick cooking spray. Preheat over medium heat. Add vegetables; cook and stir until crisp-tender.

3. Spread pizza sauce onto pita bread rounds; top with vegetables and cheese. Bake for 8 to 10 minutes more or until light brown. Cut each round into 4 wedges. Serve warm. Makes 4 (2-wedge) servings.

Vegetable Pita Pizzas

Rosemary Roasted Nuts

Aromatic rosemary brings a pleasant evergreen flavor to nutty nibble. Fill bags with some for guests to take home.

PER 1/4-CUP SERVING: 198 cal., 20 g total fat (2 g sat. fat), 0 mg chol., 102 mg sodium, 4 g carb., 2 g fiber, 5 g pro. Exchanges: 1 high-fat meat, 2 fat. Carb choices: 0.

Nonstick cooking spray
- 1 egg white
- 2 teaspoons snipped fresh rosemary or 1 teaspoon dried rosemary, crushed
- 1/2 teaspoon salt
- 1/2 teaspoon ground black pepper
- 3 cups walnut pieces, hazelnuts (filberts), and/or whole almonds

1. Preheat oven to 350°F. Line a 13×9×2-inch baking pan with foil; lightly coat foil with nonstick cooking spray. Set aside. In a medium bowl, use a fork to lightly beat egg white until frothy. Add rosemary, salt, and pepper; beat until combined. Add nuts; toss gently to coat.

2. Spread nut mixture in an even layer in the prepared baking pan. Bake for 15 to 20 minutes or until golden, stirring once.

3. Remove foil with nuts from pan; set aside to cool. Break up large pieces. Makes 12 (1/4-cup) servings.

Test Kitchen Tip: Store nuts in an airtight container in the freezer for up to 1 month.

Rosemary Roasted Nuts

Mini Spinach Calzones

Reduced-fat cream cheese adds flavor without all the fat.

PER CALZONE: 56 cal., 2 g total fat (1 g sat. fat), 4 mg chol., 125 mg sodium, 8 g carb., 0 g fiber, 2 g pro. Exchanges: 0.5 starch, 0.5 fat. Carb choices: 0.5.

Nonstick cooking spray
- 1/2 of a 10-ounce package frozen chopped spinach, thawed and well drained
- 1/2 of an 8-ounce package reduced-fat cream cheese (Neufchâtel), softened
- 3 tablespoons grated Parmesan cheese
- 2 tablespoons chopped green onions
- 1/4 teaspoon ground black pepper
- 1 13.8-ounce package refrigerated pizza dough
- 1 tablespoon egg white
- 1 tablespoon water

1. Preheat oven to 400°F. Line 2 baking sheets with foil; lightly coat with cooking spray. Set aside.

2. For filling, in a medium bowl, stir together spinach, cream cheese, 2 tablespoons of the Parmesan cheese, green onions, and pepper; set aside.

3. On a lightly floured surface, unroll dough; roll to 15-inch square. Cut into twenty-five 3-inch squares.

4. For each, spoon a slightly rounded teaspoon filling onto each square. In a small bowl, combine egg white and the water; brush onto edges. Lift a corner; stretch over filling to opposite corner, making a triangle. Use a fork to seal edges.

5. On prepared sheet, arrange calzones. Prick tops. Brush with egg white mixture. Sprinkle with the remaining 1 tablespoon Parmesan cheese. Bake for 8 to 10 minutes or until golden. Makes 25 calzones.

Make-Ahead Directions: Prepare the filling; cover and chill in the refrigerator for up to 24 hours.

Feta and Pine Nut Spirals

When you need an appetizer in a hurry, skip the pizza dough and make a dip from the cheesy Mediterranean-style filling, adding a little extra milk. Serve it with precut vegetable dippers from your supermarket's salad bar.

PER SLICE: 87 cal., 4 g total fat (2 g sat. fat), 7 mg chol., 163 mg sodium, 10 g carb., 0 g fiber, 3 g pro. Exchanges: 1 starch. Carb choices: 1.

Nonstick cooking spray

1   3-ounce package reduced-fat cream cheese (Neufchâtel), softened

½   cup crumbled feta cheese with garlic and herb (2 ounces)

3   tablespoons toasted pine nuts or chopped toasted almonds

3   tablespoons finely chopped pitted, ripe olives

2   tablespoons snipped fresh parsley

1   tablespoon fat-free milk

1   13.8-ounce package refrigerated pizza dough

Olive oil

Ground black pepper

1. Preheat oven to 375°F. Coat a baking sheet with nonstick cooking spray; set aside. For filling, in a small bowl, stir together cream cheese, feta cheese, nuts, olives, parsley, and milk; set aside.

2. On a lightly floured surface, roll pizza dough into a 14×10-inch rectangle. Cut dough in half crosswise to form two 10×7-inch rectangles. Spread half of the filling onto each dough rectangle to within 1 inch of edges. Starting from a long side, roll up each rectangle into a spiral. Seal seams and ends. Place spirals, seam sides down, on prepared baking sheet. Brush surfaces of spirals with oil; sprinkle with pepper.

3. Bake for 18 to 20 minutes or until golden. Cool on baking sheet on a wire rack for 5 minutes. Using a serrated knife, cut spirals into 1-inch-thick slices. Serve warm. Makes 20 slices.

cozy, comforting breakfasts

Tex-Mex Spinach Omelet

When *family comes* to stay for Christmas or New Year's, wake everyone in the house with the *tempting aroma* of freshly baked scones and just-brewed coffee. Once the kids are out of bed, *invite them to sit down* to a steaming stack of pancakes or French toast. *What a way to start* the holiday!

Tex-Mex Spinach Omelet

A colorful corn relish brightens an otherwise simple dish.

PER SERVING: 142 cal., 5 g total fat (3 g sat. fat), 12 mg chol., 393 mg sodium, 9 g carb., 2 g fiber, 17 g pro. Exchanges: 2 very lean meat, 1.5 vegetable, 1 fat. Carb choices: 0.5.

1 cup refrigerated or frozen egg product, thawed, or 4 eggs
1 tablespoon snipped fresh cilantro
Dash salt
Dash ground cumin
Nonstick cooking spray
¼ cup shredded Monterey Jack cheese with jalapeño chile peppers, reduced-fat cheddar cheese, or reduced-fat Swiss cheese
¾ cup fresh baby spinach leaves
1 recipe Corn-Pepper Relish (see below)

1. In a medium bowl, combine egg, cilantro, salt, and cumin. Use a wire whisk to beat until frothy.

2. Coat an unheated 10-inch nonstick skillet with flared sides with nonstick cooking spray. Preheat skillet over medium heat.

3. Pour egg mixture into prepared skillet. Cook, without stirring, for 2 to 3 minutes or until it begins to set. Run a spatula around edge, lifting mixture so uncooked portion flows underneath. Continue cooking until egg is set but still glossy and moist.

4. Sprinkle with cheese. Top with three-fourths of the spinach and half of the Corn-Pepper Relish. Using the spatula, lift and fold an edge of omelet over filling. Top with remaining spinach and relish. To serve, cut omelet in half. Makes 2 servings.

Corn-Pepper Relish: In a small bowl, combine ¼ cup chopped red sweet pepper; ¼ cup frozen whole kernel corn, thawed; 2 tablespoons chopped red onion; and 1 tablespoon snipped fresh cilantro. Makes ¾ cup.

Asparagus-Zucchini Frittata

Not to worry if asparagus isn't in season. Just use a couple of packages of frozen asparagus instead.

PER SERVING: 129 cal., 7 g total fat (2 g sat. fat), 266 mg chol., 467 mg sodium, 6 g carb., 1 g fiber, 11 g pro. Exchanges: 1 medium-fat meat, 1 vegetable, 0.5 fat. Carb choices: 0.5.

Nonstick cooking spray
- 1½ pounds fresh asparagus, trimmed and cut into 2-inch-long pieces, or two 9- or 10-ounce packages frozen cut asparagus
- 1 medium yellow sweet pepper, cut into ¼-inch-wide strips
- ⅓ cup chopped onion
- 2 tablespoons bottled roasted red sweet peppers, drained
- 1 small zucchini, halved lengthwise and cut into ¼-inch-thick slices (about 1 cup)
- 10 eggs or 2½ cups refrigerated or frozen egg product, thawed
- 1 cup fat-free milk
- 1 tablespoon snipped fresh dill or 1 teaspoon dried dillweed
- 1¼ teaspoons salt
- ¼ to ½ teaspoon ground black pepper
  Fresh dill sprigs (optional)

1. Preheat oven to 350°F. Coat a 2-quart rectangular baking dish with nonstick cooking spray; set aside.

2. In a saucepan, cook asparagus, yellow sweet pepper strips, and onion in a small amount of boiling water about 1 minute or until crisp-tender. Drain well. Stir in roasted red sweet peppers.

3. In the prepared baking dish, spread asparagus-pepper mixture evenly. Layer zucchini slices on top.

4. In a large bowl, use a wire whisk to beat eggs. Stir in milk, snipped dill, salt, and black pepper. Pour over the vegetables in baking dish.

5. Bake mixture, uncovered, about 35 minutes or until a knife inserted near center comes out clean. Let stand for 10 minutes before serving. Cut into squares. If desired, garnish with dill sprigs. Makes 8 servings.

Hash Brown Strata

A strata makes a perfect breakfast—
everything you need is in one dish.
Just as good: Mix ahead, chill, and bake in the morning.

PER SERVING: 162 cal., 5 g total fat (2 g sat. fat), 17 mg chol., 477 mg sodium, 15 g carb., 1 g fiber, 15 g pro. Exchanges: 1 starch, 2 very lean meat. Carb choices: 1.

Nonstick cooking spray
2   cups loose-pack frozen diced hash brown potatoes with onion and peppers
1   cup broccoli florets
3   ounces turkey bacon or turkey ham, cooked and chopped or crumbled
⅓   cup evaporated fat-free milk
2   tablespoons all-purpose flour
2   8-ounce cartons refrigerated or frozen egg product, thawed, or 8 eggs, beaten
½   cup shredded reduced-fat cheddar cheese (2 ounces)
1   tablespoon snipped fresh basil or ½ teaspoon dried basil, crushed
¼   teaspoon ground black pepper
⅛   teaspoon salt

1. Preheat oven to 350°F. Coat a 2-quart square baking dish with nonstick cooking spray. Spread hash brown potatoes and broccoli evenly in bottom of prepared baking dish; top with turkey bacon. Set aside.

2. In a medium bowl, slowly stir milk into flour. Stir in egg, half of the cheese, the basil, pepper, and salt; pour over vegetables.

3. Bake, uncovered, for 40 to 45 minutes or until a knife inserted near the center comes out clean. Sprinkle with remaining cheese. Let stand for 5 minutes before serving. Cut into triangles. Makes 6 servings.

Make-Ahead Directions: Prepare as directed through Step 2. Cover and chill for 4 to 24 hours. Preheat oven to 350°F. Continue as in Step 3.

Fresh Tomato Omelets with Mozzarella Cheese

Fresh Tomato Omelets with Mozzarella Cheese

To serve more, make the recipe two or three times. For a flavor change, substitute basil or thyme for the oregano.

PER SERVING: 103 cal., 2 g total fat (1 g sat. fat), 9 mg chol., 463 mg sodium, 4 g carb., 1 g fiber, 16 g pro. Exchanges: 0.5 vegetable, 2 very lean meat, 0.5 fat. Carb choices: 0.

1   cup refrigerated or frozen egg product, thawed, or 4 eggs, beaten
⅛   teaspoon salt
⅛   teaspoon ground black pepper
Nonstick cooking spray
1   teaspoon snipped fresh oregano or ¼ teaspoon dried oregano, crushed
4   medium tomato slices
¼   cup shredded mozzarella cheese (1 ounce)
Small tomato, cut into wedges (optional)

1. In a small bowl, stir together egg, salt, and pepper. Coat an unheated 8-inch nonstick skillet with nonstick cooking spray. Preheat skillet over medium heat.

2. Pour ½ cup of the egg mixture into the hot skillet. Immediately begin stirring egg mixture gently but continuously with a wooden or plastic spatula until mixture resembles small pieces of cooked egg surrounded by liquid egg. Stop stirring. Cook for 30 to 60 seconds more or until egg is set but shiny.

3. Sprinkle half of the fresh oregano or half of the dried oregano onto the eggs. Place 2 slices of tomato on top of one half of the egg mixture in skillet. Top with half of the shredded cheese.

4. Use a spatula to lift and fold the opposite edge of the omelet over tomatoes. Flip or slide omelet onto a warm plate; keep warm. Repeat with remaining egg mixture, oregano, tomato, and cheese. If desired top with tomato wedges. Makes 2 servings.

Rosemary Potato Frittata

To cut the fat, you cook the potatoes and onions in water instead of sautéeing them in butter.

PER SERVING: 168 cal., 4 g total fat (3 g sat. fat), 13 mg chol., 407 mg sodium, 15 g carb., 2 g fiber, 17 g pro. Exchanges: 1 starch, 2 very lean meat, 0.5 fat. Carb choices: 1.

    4 ounces tiny new potatoes, cut into ¼-inch
       slices (1 cup)
    ¼ cup chopped red or yellow onion
    ¼ cup chopped red, green, and/or yellow sweet pepper
    1 cup refrigerated or frozen egg product, thawed, or
       4 eggs
    ½ teaspoon snipped fresh rosemary or
       ¼ teaspoon dried rosemary, crushed
    ⅛ teaspoon salt
    ⅛ teaspoon ground black pepper
       Nonstick cooking spray
    ¼ cup shredded Swiss cheese (1 ounce)
       Fresh rosemary (optional)

1. In a covered 6- to 7-inch nonstick skillet with flared sides, cook potatoes and onion in a small amount of boiling water for 7 minutes. Add sweet pepper. Cook, covered, for 3 to 5 minutes more or until vegetables are tender. Drain in a colander.

2. Meanwhile, in a small bowl, whisk together egg, ½ teaspoon rosemary, salt, and pepper. Set aside.

3. Wipe out skillet; lightly coat with cooking spray. Return vegetables to skillet. Pour egg mixture over vegetables. Cook over medium heat, without stirring, about 1 minute or until egg mixture begins to set. Run a spatula around the edge, lifting mixture so uncooked portion flows underneath. Continue cooking and lifting edges until egg is almost set but still glossy and moist.

4. Remove skillet from heat. Sprinkle with cheese. Let stand, covered, for 3 to 4 minutes or until top is set and cheese is melted.

5. To serve, cut frittata into wedges. If desired, top each serving with fresh rosemary. Makes 2 servings.

Breakfast Tortilla Wrap

Turkey bacon, refrigerated or frozen egg product, and a whole wheat tortilla add up to an extra lean, extra delicious breakfast in a bundle.

PER SERVING: 209 cal., 5 g total fat (1 g sat. fat), 10 mg chol., 687 mg sodium, 29 g carb., 3 g fiber, 12 g pro. Exchanges: 2 starch, 1 very lean meat. Carb choices: 2.

    1 slice turkey bacon
       Nonstick cooking spray
    2 tablespoons chopped green sweet pepper
    ⅛ teaspoon ground cumin
    ⅛ teaspoon crushed red pepper (optional)
    ¼ cup refrigerated or frozen egg product, thawed, or
       2 egg whites, slightly beaten
    2 tablespoons chopped tomato
    3 dashes bottled hot pepper sauce (optional)
    1 8-inch whole wheat tortilla, warmed*

1. Prepare turkey bacon according to package directions; crumble and set aside.

2. Coat a medium nonstick skillet with nonstick cooking spray. Heat skillet over medium heat; add sweet pepper, cumin, and, if desired, crushed red pepper. Cook and stir until sweet pepper is tender, about 3 minutes. Add egg; cook, without stirring, until mixture begins to set on the bottom and around edge. With a spatula or large spoon, lift and fold the partially cooked egg mixture so that the uncooked portion flows underneath. Continue cooking for 2 to 3 minutes or until egg mixture is cooked through but is still glossy and moist.

3. Stir in bacon, tomato, and, if desired, hot pepper sauce. Spoon onto tortilla; roll up. Makes 1 serving.

*Test Kitchen Tip: Wrap tortilla in white microwave-safe paper towels; microwave on high for 15 to 30 seconds or until softened. (Or preheat oven to 350°F. Wrap tortilla in foil. Heat in oven for 10 to 15 minutes or until warm.)

Rosemary Potato Frittata

Quick Tip:

Refrigerated or frozen
egg substitutes are readily
available. Based mostly on
egg whites, they contain less
fat than whole eggs and no
cholesterol. Use ¼ cup of
egg product for each large
egg in scrambled egg dishes,
omelets, quiches,
and stratas.

Breakfast Tortilla Wrap

Ginger Pear Muffins

(oat health notes)

Oats may help fight off many diseases, including these:

Diabetes: Studies show eating whole grains such as oats can significantly lower your risk of obesity and diabetes. What's more, consuming more whole grains can improve insulin sensitivity for people with insulin resistance or type 2 diabetes. That means insulin will respond more efficiently to high blood glucose levels. Oats and other fiber-rich foods help keep blood glucose stable throughout the day when eaten for breakfast.

Heart disease: Oats and oat products contain a type of fiber called beta-glucan, which has been shown to help lower cholesterol. Antioxidants in oats called avenanthramides help keep LDL (bad) cholesterol from oxidizing, especially when you consume oats with vitamin C. For an extra heart health benefit, eat a grapefruit half or drink orange juice with your morning oats.

Cancer: Oats are a good source of selenium, which is involved in the DNA repair associated with reducing the risk of cancer, especially of the colon. They also help decrease asthma symptoms.

Best-of-Bran Muffins

Best-of-Bran Muffins

These muffins are stuffed with good things: fiber-rich bran, flaxseeds, and canola oil.

PER MUFFIN: 146 cal., 6 g total fat (0 g sat. fat), 1 mg chol., 188 mg sodium, 23 g carb., 4 g fiber, 4 g pro. Exchanges: 1 starch, 0.5 carb., 1 fat. Carb choices: 1.5.

- 3 cups whole bran cereal (not flakes)
- 1 cup tropical blend or regular mixed dried fruit bits or raisins
- ½ cup ground flaxseeds
- ½ cup canola oil or cooking oil
- 1 cup boiling water
- 2 cups buttermilk
- ½ cup refrigerated or frozen egg product, thawed, or 2 eggs, slightly beaten
- ¼ cup molasses
- 2¼ cups whole wheat flour
- ½ cup chopped walnuts (optional)
- 1 tablespoon sugar
- 2½ teaspoons baking soda
   Nonstick cooking spray

1. In a very large bowl, combine cereal, dried fruit, flaxseeds, and oil. Pour boiling water over mixture. Let stand for 5 minutes.

2. In a medium bowl, combine buttermilk, egg, and molasses; add to bran mixture. Stir to combine.

3. In a bowl, stir together flour, nuts (if using), sugar, and baking soda; add to bran mixture. Stir just until moistened (do not overmix). Let stand for 15 to 30 minutes.

4. Meanwhile, preheat oven to 400°F. Lightly coat twenty-four 2½-inch muffin cups with nonstick cooking spray. Spoon batter into prepared cups, filling each about three-fourths full. Bake 15 minutes or until a toothpick inserted in centers comes out clean. Cool in cups on wire racks for 5 minutes. Remove from cups. Serve warm. Makes 24 muffins.

Ginger Pear Muffins

Sprinkle on a little spiced oat bran for a streusellike topper.

PER MUFFIN: 149 cal., 7 g total fat (1 g sat. fat), 0 mg chol., 96 mg sodium, 19 g carb., 2 g fiber, 3 g pro. Exchanges: 1 starch, 1.5 fat. Carb choices: 1.

PER MUFFIN WITH SUBSTITUTE: same as above, except 136 cal., 16 g carb.

   Nonstick cooking spray
- 1 cup all-purpose flour
- 1 cup quick-cooking rolled oats
- 3 tablespoons packed brown sugar or brown sugar substitute* equivalent to 3 tablespoons brown sugar
- 1½ teaspoons baking powder
- ½ teaspoon ground ginger
- ¼ teaspoon salt
- ¼ cup refrigerated or frozen egg product, thawed, or 1 egg
- ⅔ cup fat-free milk
- ⅓ cup cooking oil
- ¾ cup chopped, cored pear
- ¼ cup chopped walnuts (optional)
- 1 tablespoon oat bran
- ¼ teaspoon ground ginger

1. Preheat oven to 400°F. Lightly coat twelve 2½-inch muffin cups with cooking spray; set aside.

2. In a large bowl, stir together flour, rolled oats, brown sugar, baking powder, the ½ teaspoon ginger, and the salt. Make a well in the center.

3. In a small bowl, beat egg; stir in milk and oil. Add all at once to flour mixture. Using a fork, stir just until moistened (batter should be lumpy). Fold in chopped pear and, if desired, walnuts.

4. Divide batter among prepared muffin cups. Combine oat bran and the ¼ teaspoon ginger; sprinkle onto muffins. Bake for 18 to 20 minutes or until golden.

5. Cool muffins in muffin cups on a wire rack for 5 minutes. Remove from muffin cups; serve warm. Makes 12 muffins.

*Sugar Substitutes: Choose from 1½ teaspoons Sweet'N Low Brown or 3 tablespoons Sugar Twin Granulated Brown in place of the brown sugar.

Tangerine Puckers

These mini muffins are sized just right for brunch.

PER MINI MUFFIN: 43 cal., 1 g total fat (0 g sat. fat), 0 mg chol., 59 mg sodium, 8 g carb., 0 g fiber, 1 g pro. Exchanges: 0.5 other carb. Carb choices: 0.5.

PER MINI MUFFIN WITH SUBSTITUTE: same as above, except 38 cal., 6 g carb.

Nonstick cooking spray
1 cup all-purpose flour
1½ teaspoons baking powder
2 tablespoons sugar or sugar substitute* equivalent to 2 tablespoons sugar
¼ teaspoon salt
2 tablespoons refrigerated or frozen egg product, thawed, or 1 egg white
½ cup fat-free milk
1 tablespoon cooking oil
1 teaspoon vanilla
½ cup fresh tangerine sections (2 to 3 tangerines), coarsely chopped

1. Preheat oven to 400°F. Lightly coat eighteen 1¾-inch muffin cups with nonstick spray; set aside.

2. In a medium bowl, stir together flour, baking powder, sugar, and salt. Make a well in the center of the flour mixture; set aside.

3. In a bowl, beat egg; stir in milk, oil, and vanilla. Add all at once to flour mixture. Using a fork, stir just until moistened (batter should be lumpy). Fold in the tangerine sections.

4. Divide batter among prepared cups, filling each almost full. Bake about 14 minutes or until golden.

5. Cool in muffin cups on a wire rack for 5 minutes. Remove from cups. Makes 18 mini muffins.

*Sugar Substitutes: Choose from Splenda granular, Equal Spoonful or packets, or Sweet'N Low bulk or packets. Follow package directions to measure the product amount equivalent to 2 tablespoons sugar.

Lemon-Nutmeg Scones

Try these first with the lemon yogurt, then next time substitute orange or peach yogurt for the lemon.

PER MINI SCONE: 173 cal., 7 g total fat (3 g sat. fat), 16 mg chol., 206 mg sodium, 26 g carb., 2 g fiber, 5 g pro. Exchanges: 1 carb., 1 starch. Carb choices: 2.

PER MINI SCONE WITH SUBSTITUTE: same as above, except 156 cal., 22 g carb. Exchanges: 0.5 carb., Carb choices: 1.5.

Nonstick cooking spray
1¼ cups all-purpose flour
¾ cup oat bran
3 tablespoons sugar or sugar substitute* equivalent to 3 tablespoons sugar
2 teaspoons baking powder
¼ teaspoon baking soda
¼ teaspoon ground nutmeg
⅛ teaspoon salt
¼ cup butter
1 6-ounce carton lemon, orange, or peach low-fat yogurt with sweetener
¼ cup refrigerated or frozen egg product, thawed, or 1 egg

1. Preheat oven to 400°F. Lightly coat a baking sheet with nonstick spray; set aside.

2. In a medium bowl, stir together flour, oat bran, sugar, baking powder, baking soda, nutmeg, and salt. Using a pastry blender, cut in butter until crumbly. In a bowl, combine yogurt and egg; add all at once to flour mixture. Stir just until moistened.

3. Turn dough out onto a lightly floured surface. Knead by folding and gently pressing for 10 strokes. Lightly pat into a 6-inch circle. Cut dough into 8 wedges. Carefully separate wedges; place wedges about 2 inches apart on the prepared baking sheet.

4. Bake about 12 minutes or until scones are golden. Cool scones on the baking sheet on a wire rack for 5 minutes. Remove scones from the baking sheet. Serve warm. Makes 8 scones.

*Sugar Substitutes: Choose from Splenda granular, Equal Spoonful or packets, or Sweet'N Low bulk or packets. Follow package directions to measure the product amount equivalent to 3 tablespoons sugar.

(smart spreads for breads)

Before you slather butter onto your toast or bread, think about some of the delicious alternatives. By substituting some of the suggestions below in small amounts for traditional bread spreads, you can slash some of the saturated fat or sugar from your diet. (Be aware that some reduced-fat products may contain more sugar to enhance the flavor. Read the labels to check the number of carbohydrates.)

- Reduced-fat or fat-free options: peanut butter, cream cheese, margarine, Benecol (cholesterol-lowering spread)
- Reduced-sugar or low-calorie options: apple butter; spreadable fruit or fruit preserves; fruit jellies

Lemon-Nutmeg Scones

Mango Coffee Cake

If you can't find fresh mango, use a jar of mango slices instead. You'll find them in the refrigerated area in the produce section of your supermarket.

PER SERVING: 208 cal., 6 g total fat (1 g sat. fat), 0 mg chol., 73 mg sodium, 35 g carb., 3 g fiber, 4 g pro. Exchanges: 1 starch, 1½ carb., 1 fat. Carb choices: 2.

PER SERVING WITH SUBSTITUTE: same as above, except 190 cal., 30 g carb. Exchanges: 1 carb.

Nonstick cooking spray
2 medium fresh mangoes
½ cup sugar or sugar substitute-sugar blend equivalent to ½ cup sugar*
¼ cup cooking oil
¾ cup fat-free milk
⅓ cup refrigerated or frozen egg product, thawed, or 2 egg whites
⅔ cup all-purpose flour
½ cup whole wheat flour
2 teaspoons baking powder
½ teaspoon finely shredded lime peel
¼ teaspoon ground cardamom or ground allspice
1¼ cups quick-cooking rolled oats

1. Preheat oven to 375°F. Lightly coat a 9×1½-inch round baking pan with nonstick cooking spray; set aside. Seed, peel, and chop one of the mangoes; set aside. Seed, peel, and slice the remaining mango; set aside.

2. In a large bowl, stir together sugar and oil. Add milk and egg. Beat with an electric mixer on medium speed for 1 minute. In a small bowl, combine all-purpose flour, whole wheat flour, baking powder, lime peel, and cardamom. Add to egg mixture; beat until combined. Stir in chopped mango and oats. Spoon into prepared pan. Arrange sliced mango on top of batter.

3. Bake for 35 to 40 minutes or until a toothpick inserted near the center of the cake comes out clean. Cool in pan on a wire rack for 30 minutes. Remove from pan. Serve warm. Makes 10 servings.

*Test Kitchen Tip: If using a sugar substitute-sugar blend, we recommend Splenda Sugar Blend for Baking or Equal Sugar Lite. Be sure to use package directions to determine product amount equivalent to ½ cup sugar.

Cranberry Whole Wheat Scones

A sprinkle of rolled oats decorates the tops and adds a little fiber to these merry treats.

PER SCONE: 169 cal., 6 g total fat (3 g sat. fat), 15 mg chol., 172 mg sodium, 26 g carb., 2 g fiber, 4 g pro. Exchanges: 1 starch, 0.5 fruit, 0.5 carb., 1 fat. Carb choices: 2.

PER SCONE WITH SUBSTITUTE: same as above, except 157 cal., 23 g carb. Exchanges: 0 carb. Carb choices: 1.5.

1½ cups all-purpose flour
½ cup whole wheat flour
3 tablespoons sugar or sugar substitute* equivalent to 3 tablespoons sugar
1½ teaspoons baking powder
1 teaspoon ground ginger or cinnamon
¼ teaspoon baking soda
¼ teaspoon salt
⅓ cup butter
½ cup refrigerated or frozen egg product, thawed, or 2 eggs
⅓ cup buttermilk
¾ cup dried cranberries or currants
Buttermilk
3 tablespoons rolled oats

1. Preheat oven to 400°F. In a large bowl, stir together all-purpose flour, whole wheat flour, sugar, baking powder, ginger, baking soda, and salt. Using a pastry blender, cut in the butter until mixture resembles coarse crumbs. Make a well in the center of flour mixture; set aside.

2. In a small bowl, beat egg slightly; stir in the ⅓ cup buttermilk and cranberries. Add buttermilk mixture all at once to flour mixture. Stir just until moistened (some of the dough may look dry).

3. Turn out dough onto a floured surface. Knead dough for 10 to 12 strokes or until nearly smooth. Pat or lightly roll dough to an 8-inch circle about ¾ inch thick. Brush top with additional buttermilk; sprinkle with oats, pressing gently into dough. Cut into 12 wedges.

4. Place dough wedges 1 inch apart on an ungreased baking sheet. Bake for 13 to 15 minutes or until edges are light brown. Serve warm. Makes 12 scones.

*Sugar Substitutes: Choose from Splenda granular, Equal Spoonful or packets, or Sweet'N Low packets or bulk. Follow package directions to use product amount equivalent to 3 tablespoons sugar.

Clockwise from top: **Spiced Irish Oatmeal,
Toasted Oat Muesli,** and **Double Oat Granola**

Toasted Oat Muesli

You'll find flaxseeds, rich in omega-3 fatty acids,
in the natural food aisle.

PER SERVING: 231 cal., 10 g total fat (3 g sat. fat), 2 mg chol., 57 mg sodium,
27 g carb., 5 g fiber, 10 g pro. Exchanges: 0.5 fruit, 1 starch, 0.5 fat-free
milk, 1.5 fat. Carb choices: 1.5.

1½ **cups rolled oats**
½ **cup sliced almonds, coarsely chopped**
3 **tablespoons flaxseeds**
½ **cup dried banana chips and/or raisins**
½ **teaspoon ground allspice or ground cinnamon**
3½ **cups fat-free milk**

1. Preheat oven to 350°F. Place oats in a 15×10×1-inch
baking pan. Bake for 8 minutes

2. Stir in almonds and flaxseeds. Bake for 8 to
10 minutes more or until oats are light brown and
almonds are toasted, stirring once.

3. Cool in pan on a wire rack. Add banana chips and
allspice; stir to combine. Serve with milk. Makes
7 (⅓-cup) servings.

Make-Ahead Directions: Cover and refrigerate for up to
2 weeks.

Double Oat Granola

Enjoy granola as a cereal with milk or yogurt
or bake it into fruity bars for quick snacks.

PER SERVING: 175 cal., 6 g total fat (1 g sat. fat), 0 mg chol., 29 mg sodium,
27 g carb., 4 g fiber, 5 g pro. Exchanges: 1 starch, 1 carb., 0.5 fat. Carb
choices: 2.
PER BAR: 93 cal., 4 g total fat (1 g sat. fat), 9 mg chol., 11 mg sodium,
13 g carb., 1 g fiber, 2 g pro. Exchanges: 0.5 starch, 0.5 carb., 0.5 fat.
Carb choices: 1.

    Nonstick cooking spray
2½ cups regular rolled oats
  1 cup toasted oat bran cereal
½ cup toasted wheat germ
⅓ cup pecans, coarsely chopped
½ cup unsweetened applesauce
  2 tablespoons honey
  1 tablespoon cooking oil
¼ teaspoon ground cinnamon
⅓ cup snipped dried cranberries, snipped dried tart
    cherries, and/or dried blueberries

1. Preheat oven to 325°F. Lightly coat a 15×10×1-inch
baking pan with nonstick cooking spray; set aside.

2. In a large bowl, stir together rolled oats, oat bran
cereal, wheat germ, and pecans. In a small bowl, stir
together applesauce, honey, oil, and cinnamon; pour over
cereal mixture. Stir to mix evenly.

3. Spread granola evenly onto the prepared pan. Bake
about 40 minutes or until golden brown, stirring every
10 minutes.

4. Stir dried fruit into granola. Spread on foil to cool.
Makes 10 (½-cup) servings.

Apricot Granola Bars: Preheat oven to 325°F. Line an
8×8×2-inch baking pan with foil. Lightly coat with
nonstick cooking spray. In a large bowl, combine 3 cups
Double Oat Granola, ½ cup all-purpose flour, and ¼ cup
snipped dried apricots. In a medium bowl, stir together
1 egg, ⅓ cup honey, ¼ cup cooking oil, and ½ teaspoon
apple pie spice; stir into granola mixture until coated.
Press into prepared pan. Bake about 25 minutes or until
brown on edges. Cool on a wire rack. Use foil to remove
from pan. Cut into bars. Makes 24 bars.

Make-Ahead Directions: Prepare granola or granola
bars as directed. Store in an airtight container in a cool,
dark place for up to 2 weeks.

Quick Tip:

Fruity beverages labeled as
punch, drink, or cocktail
often contain added sugars
and little fruit juice. For
the most nutrition, fill your
juice glass with 100-percent
fruit juice. Keep portion
size in mind—¼ cup of the
unsweetened fruit juice
equals 1 fruit exchange
or 1 serving.

Spiced Irish Oatmeal

Steel-cut oats may also be called Irish,
Scottish, or pinhead oats.

PER BAR: 158 cal., 2 g total fat (0 g sat. fat), 2 mg chol., 106 mg sodium,
27 g carb., 3 g fiber, 9 g pro. Exchanges: 0.5 fat-free milk,
1.5 starch. Carb choices: 2.
PER SERVING WITH SUBSTITUTE: same as above, except 149 cal.,
24 g carb. Carb choices: 1.5.

  3 cups water
  1 cup steel-cut oats
  1 tablespoon packed brown sugar or brown sugar
    substitute* equivalent to 1 tablespoon brown sugar
¼ teaspoon ground cinnamon
⅛ teaspoon salt
⅛ teaspoon ground allspice
    Dash ground cloves or ground nutmeg
  3 cups fat-free milk

1. In a 2-quart saucepan, combine water, oats, brown
sugar, cinnamon, salt, allspice, and cloves.

2. Bring to boiling; reduce heat. Simmer, uncovered,
for 10 to 15 minutes or until desired doneness and
consistency, stirring occasionally. Serve with milk. Makes
6 (½-cup) servings.

***Sugar Substitutes:** Use 1½ teaspoons Sweet'N Low
Brown or 1 tablespoon Sugar Twin Granulated Brown for
the brown sugar.

Spiced Hot Cereal

Make your usual hot cereal a spicy treat.
Choose either wheat cereal or, for more fiber, oatmeal.

PER SERVING: 149 cal., 0 g total fat (0 g sat. fat), 2 mg chol., 53 mg sodium, 31 g carb., 1 g fiber, 6 g pro. Exchanges: 0.5 starch, 0.5 carb., 0.5 fruit, 0.5 fat-free milk. Carb choices: 2.

PER SERVING WITH SUBSTITUTE: same as above, except 125 cal., 26 g carb. Exchanges: 0 carb.

- 2 cups fat-free milk
- 2 tablespoons sugar or sugar substitute* equivalent to 2 tablespoons sugar
- ⅓ cup quick-cooking wheat cereal (farina)
- ¼ cup raisins
- 1 teaspoon ground cinnamon
- Ground cinnamon (optional)

Spiced Hot Cereal

1. In a medium saucepan, combine milk and sugar. Bring milk mixture just to boiling; reduce heat. Add cereal, stirring constantly. Stir in the raisins and the 1 teaspoon cinnamon.

2. Cook, uncovered, for 2 to 3 minutes or until thickened, stirring frequently. Serve warm. If desired, sprinkle with additional cinnamon. Makes 4 (½-cup) servings.

Spiced Oatmeal: Prepare as directed, except substitute 1 cup quick-cooking rolled oats for the wheat cereal.

*****Sugar Substitutes:** Choose from Splenda granular, Equal Spoonful or packets, or Sweet'N Low bulk or packets. Follow the package directions to use the product amount equivalent to 2 tablespoons sugar.

Fruit and Yogurt Parfaits

Use kiwifruit and mango for
a green and gold combination.

PER SERVING: 181 cal., 4 g total fat (1 g sat. fat), 7 mg chol., 88 mg sodium, 30 g carb., 4 g fiber, 9 g pro. Exchanges: 1 fat-free milk, 0.5 fruit, 0.5 starch, 0.5 fat. Carb choices: 2.

- 1 medium fresh mango, peach, or nectarine or 2 medium kiwifruits
- 1 cup plain low-fat yogurt
- ½ teaspoon vanilla
- ½ cup bite-size shredded wheat biscuits, coarsely crushed
- 2 teaspoons sugar-free pancake and waffle syrup or light pancake and waffle syrup product
- 1 tablespoon sliced almonds, toasted
- Dash ground cinnamon

1. If desired, peel fruit; pit peach or nectarine. Chop fruit, reserving 2 wedges for garnish. Set aside.

2. Combine yogurt and vanilla. Spoon half of the yogurt mixture into two 8- to 10-ounce parfait glasses. Top with half of the crushed cereal, all of the chopped fruit, syrup, remaining yogurt mixture, and remaining crushed cereal. Sprinkle with almonds and cinnamon. Garnish each serving with a reserved fruit wedge. Makes 2 (¾-cup) servings.

(order up!)

Want a preshopping breakfast at your favorite diner? Use these tips to follow your meal plan.

1. Look for the light. Check the menu for a section listing low-fat or lightened dishes.

2. Be wise about size. With large portions, request half an order or an empty plate to share.

3. Order egg options. Request egg dishes be made with egg product instead of whole eggs.

4. Select lean meat. If ordering meat, choose lean ham, Canadian bacon, or turkey bacon.

5. Choose the right sides. Substitute fresh fruit for hash browns. Ask that the toast be whole grain.

6. Make sides the mainstay. Consider whether a couple of sides can become your meal, such as a small bran muffin with yogurt and fruit.

7. Skip butter. Top pancakes with sugar-free syrup, low-sugar fruit preserves, yogurt, or berries.

Fruit and Yogurt Parfaits

Tropical Fruit Smoothies

Tropical Fruit Smoothies

These do double duty as a quick breakfast
or a nutritious dessert.

PER SERVING: 103 cal., 0 g total fat (0 g sat. fat), 2 mg chol., 53 mg sodium,
22 g carb., 2 g fiber, 5 g pro. Exchanges: 0.5 fruit, 0.5 fat-free milk,
0.5 carb. Carb choices: 1.5.

1 6-ounce carton apricot-mango, orange-mango, piña
   colada, or pineapple fat-free yogurt with sweetener
1 cup fat-free milk
1 cup sliced fresh banana
1 cup sliced fresh mango or refrigerated mango slices
1 cup small ice cubes or crushed ice
   Sliced mango, lime wedges, or pineapple wedges
   (optional)

1. In a blender, combine yogurt, milk, banana, and
1 cup sliced mango. Cover; blend until smooth. With
blender running, add ice cubes through hole in lid, one
at a time, until smooth. If desired, garnish with mango,
lime, or pineapple. Makes 4 (1-cup) servings.

Strawberry-Banana Smoothies

Remember this recipe when you're short on time.

PER SERVING: 108 cal., 2 g total fat (0 g sat. fat), 2 mg chol., 30 mg sodium,
24 g carb., 4 g fiber, 4 g pro. Exchanges: 4 fruit. Carb choices: 2.

4 cups sliced fresh strawberries
1 medium banana, sliced
1 6-ounce carton vanilla low-fat yogurt
1 cup ice cubes
1 kiwifruit, peeled and sliced (optional)

1. In a blender, combine strawberries, banana, and
yogurt; cover and blend until smooth. With blender
running, add ice cubes, one at a time, through the hole
in the lid, until smooth. If desired, garnish each serving
with kiwifruit. Makes 4 (1-cup) servings.

Quick Tip:

Yogurts that list "active
yogurt cultures" or "living
yogurt cultures" on the label
help to replenish the so-
called friendly bacteria in
your intestines if the supply
dwindles. This decrease in
friendly bacteria occurs due
to age, illness, or the use of
medications, such
as antibiotics.

Blueberry Buckwheat Pancakes

Buckwheat contains a phytochemical that might have a beneficial effect on blood glucose levels.

PER SERVING: 132 cal., 3 g total fat (1 g sat. fat), 2 mg chol., 244 mg sodium, 22 g carb., 3 g fiber, 6 g pro. Exchanges: 1 starch, 0.5 carb., 0.5 fat. Carb choices: 1.5.

½ cup buckwheat flour
½ cup whole wheat flour
1 tablespoon sugar
½ teaspoon baking powder
¼ teaspoon baking soda
¼ teaspoon salt
¼ cup refrigerated or frozen egg product, thawed, or 1 egg
1¼ cups buttermilk or sour milk
1 tablespoon cooking oil
¼ teaspoon vanilla
¾ cup fresh or frozen blueberries, thawed

1. In a medium bowl, stir together buckwheat flour, whole wheat flour, sugar, baking powder, baking soda, and salt. Make a well in center; set aside.

2. In a small bowl, beat egg slightly; stir in buttermilk, oil, and vanilla. Add buttermilk mixture all at once to flour mixture. Stir just until combined but still slightly lumpy. Stir in blueberries.

3. Heat a lightly greased griddle or heavy skillet over medium heat until a few drops of water sprinkled onto griddle dance across the surface. For each pancake, pour a scant ¼ cup batter onto hot griddle. Spread the batter into a circle that's about 4 inches in diameter.

4. Cook over medium heat until pancakes are brown, turning to cook second sides when pancake surfaces are bubbly and edges are slightly dry (1 to 2 minutes per side). Serve immediately or keep warm. Makes 6 (2-pancake) servings.

Fruit-Filled Puff Pancakes

These puff pancakes deflate after baking to form a bowl just right for filling with fresh, colorful fruit.

PER SERVING: 163 cal., 5 g total fat (1 g sat. fat), 0 mg chol., 138 mg sodium, 26 g carb., 3 g fiber, 5 g pro. Exchanges: 1 carb., 1 fruit, 1 fat. Carb choices: 2.

  Nonstick cooking spray
¼ cup refrigerated or frozen egg product, thawed, or
   1 egg
 2 tablespoons all-purpose flour
 2 tablespoons fat-free milk
 2 teaspoons cooking oil
  Dash salt
 1 tablespoon low-calorie orange marmalade spread
 1 tablespoon orange juice or water
 1 small banana, sliced
½ cup fresh blueberries, raspberries, and/or
   sliced strawberries

1. Preheat oven to 400°F. For pancakes, coat two 4- to 5-inch pie plates or foil tart pans or 10-ounce custard cups with nonstick spray. Set aside.

2. In a medium bowl, whisk together egg, flour, milk, oil, and salt until smooth. Divide batter among prepared pans. Bake about 25 minutes or until brown and puffed. Turn off oven; let stand in oven 5 minutes.

3. Meanwhile, in a small bowl, stir together marmalade and orange juice. Add banana and berries; stir gently to coat.

4. To serve, immediately after removing pancakes from oven, transfer to plates. Spoon fruit mixture into each pancake center. Makes 2 (1-pancake) servings.

Oat Bran Pancakes

Add blueberries to these hearty pancakes, if you like. Orange peel adds another flavor option, too.

PER SERVING: 124 cal., 3 g total fat (0 g sat. fat), 1 mg chol., 199 mg sodium, 23 g carb., 1 g fiber, 4 g pro. Exchanges: 1.5 starch. Carb choices: 1.5.
PER SERVING WITH BLUEBERRIES: 128 cal., 3 g total fat (0 g sat. fat), 1 mg chol., 199 mg sodium, 24 g carb., 1 g fiber, 4 g pro. Exchanges: 1.5 starch. Carb choices: 1.5.

⅔ cup all-purpose flour
⅓ cup oat bran
 1 tablespoon packed brown sugar
 2 teaspoons baking powder
⅛ teaspoon salt
 1 cup fat-free milk
 1 tablespoon cooking oil
 2 egg whites
  Nonstick cooking spray
  Sugar-free or light pancake and waffle syrup product
   (optional)
 1 teaspoon finely shredded orange peel (optional)
  Orange wedges (optional)

1. In a bowl, stir together flour, oat bran, brown sugar, baking powder, and salt. Add milk and oil; stir just until combined.

2. In a small bowl, beat egg whites with an electric mixer on medium speed until stiff peaks form (tips stand straight). Fold egg whites into batter (small mounds of egg white will remain).

3. Lightly coat an unheated griddle or large nonstick skillet with cooking spray. Preheat over medium heat. For each pancake, spoon ¼ cup of the batter onto hot griddle; if necessary, spread to a 4-inch circle. Cook about 2 minutes on each side or until pancakes are golden, turning to second sides when pancakes have bubbly surfaces and edges are slightly dry.

4. Meanwhile, in a small saucepan, heat syrup until warm; stir in orange peel, if using. Serve syrup with pancakes. If desired, serve with orange wedges. Makes 6 (2-pancake) servings.

Blueberry Oat Bran Pancakes: Prepare as directed, except sprinkle 5 blueberries onto each pancake immediately after dropping batter onto griddle.

(10 grain ideas)

Try these ten ways to add whole grain goodness to your meals.

1. **Start your day** with whole grain cereals, oatmeal, whole grain toast, or buckwheat pancakes topped with fruit.
2. **Snack on whole grains.** Try whole grain crackers with hummus, cheese, or peanut butter. Toss whole grain cereal, nuts, and popcorn into a baggie for a snack.
3. **Slice whole grain bread,** rolls, or bagels for sandwiches at lunchtime.
4. **Cook up whole grain** pastas for favorite Italian recipes.
5. **Add cooked barley**, brown rice, or bulgur (cracked wheat) to soups, stews, or meat loaf.
6. **Substitute whole wheat** flour for up to a quarter of all-purpose flour in baking.
7. **Serve cooked grains** as side dishes, such as risotto or pilaf made with brown rice, wild rice, whole wheat couscous, barley, or quinoa.
8. **Use bulgur** or brown rice in addition to beans and veggies to make nutritious Mexican dishes.
9. **Try soba** (buckwheat) noodles or brown rice when preparing Asian dishes.
10. **Toss cooked wheat berries** into salads or add some to pasta sauce or casseroles for a chewy texture.

Fruit-Filled Puff Pancakes

Oat Buttermilk Pancakes

Oat Buttermilk Pancakes

Offer family and guests a refreshing option: sliced fresh fruit and fruit-flavored yogurt instead of syrup.

PER 2 PANCAKES: 189 cal., 5 g total fat (1 g sat. fat), 3 mg chol., 317 mg sodium, 28 g carb., 3 g fiber, 8 g pro. Exchanges: 1 starch, 1 carb., 0.5 fat. Carb choices: 2.

1¼ cups regular rolled oats
¾ cup all-purpose flour
½ cup whole wheat flour
1 tablespoon baking powder
¼ teaspoon salt
3 egg whites
2¼ cups buttermilk
2 tablespoons cooking oil
2 tablespoons honey (optional)
1 teaspoon vanilla
Nonstick cooking spray
Fresh strawberries (optional)
Light pancake and waffle syrup product (optional)

1. In a large bowl, stir together oats, all-purpose flour, whole wheat flour, baking powder, and salt. Make a well in the center; set aside.

2. In a medium bowl, use a fork to beat egg whites; stir in buttermilk, oil, honey (if using), and vanilla. Add all at once to flour mixture. Stir just until moistened (the batter should be lumpy). Cover; let stand at room temperature for 15 to 30 minutes.

3. Coat an unheated griddle or heavy skillet with nonstick cooking spray. Preheat griddle over medium-high heat.

4. For each pancake, pour about ¼ cup of the batter onto the hot griddle or skillet. Spread the batter into a 4-inch circle.

5. Cook over medium heat for 4 to 6 minutes or until pancakes are golden, turning to cook second sides when pancakes have bubbly surfaces and the edges are slightly dry.

6. If desired, garnish pancakes with strawberries sliced into fans; serve with syrup. Makes 8 (2-pancake) servings.

Walnut Waffles with Blueberry Sauce

Ground walnuts provide a light crunch and nutty flavor.

PER SERVING: 224 cal., 7 g total fat (1 g sat. fat), 3 mg chol., 359 mg sodium, 33 g carb., 4 g fiber, 8 g pro. Exchanges: 1 starch, 1 carb., 1.5 fat. Carb choices: 2.

1 cup all-purpose flour
1 cup whole wheat flour
¼ cup coarsely ground toasted walnuts
2 teaspoons baking powder
1 teaspoon baking soda
4 egg whites
2¼ cups buttermilk
2 tablespoons cooking oil
1 recipe Blueberry Sauce (see below)

1. In a medium bowl, stir together all-purpose flour, whole wheat flour, walnuts, baking powder, and soda.

2. In a bowl, beat egg whites with an electric mixer on medium speed until foamy. Stir in buttermilk and oil. Slowly add flour mixture, beating by hand until smooth. Preheat a lightly greased square or round waffle baker. Pour 1 cup batter (for round baker, use ⅔ cup batter) onto grids of square waffle baker. Close lid. Bake according to manufacturer's directions. When done, use a fork to remove waffle. Repeat with remaining batter. Serve with Blueberry Sauce. Makes 8 (3-waffle) servings.

Blueberry Sauce: In a saucepan, combine 1 cup fresh or frozen blueberries, ¼ cup white grape juice, and 1 tablespoon honey. Heat just until bubbles form around edges. Cool. Transfer to a blender. Cover; blend until smooth. Stir in 1 cup fresh or frozen blueberries. Transfer to a serving container. Makes about 1⅔ cups.

Walnut Waffles with Blueberry Sauce

Orange French Toast

If you top with sugar-free or light syrup, add those carbs to the total.

PER SERVING: 187 cal., 3 g total fat (0 g sat. fat), 1 mg chol., 250 mg sodium, 32 g carb., 8 g fiber, 12 g pro. Exchanges: 2 starch, 0.5 very lean meat. Carb choices: 1.5.

½ cup refrigerated or frozen egg product, thawed, or 2 eggs
½ cup fat-free milk
½ teaspoon finely shredded orange peel
¼ teaspoon vanilla
⅛ teaspoon ground cinnamon or nutmeg
8 slices whole grain bread
Nonstick cooking spray
Sugar-free or light pancake and waffle syrup product (optional)
Fresh blueberries and/or strawberries (optional)

1. In a shallow bowl, beat egg; stir in milk, orange peel, vanilla, and cinnamon. Dip bread slices into egg mixture, turning slices to coat both sides.

2. Coat an unheated large nonstick skillet or griddle with nonstick cooking spray. Preheat over medium heat. Place bread on hot skillet; cook for 4 to 6 minutes or until golden brown, turning once.

3. Serve warm. If desired, serve with syrup and garnish with berries. Makes 4 (2-slice) servings.

Orange French Toast

Quick Tip:

Keep these on hand to feed a crowd quickly: whole grain freezer waffles; high-protein, low-carb cereals; ingredients for smoothies; a batch of homemade bran muffins (keep them in the freezer; thaw a few at a time); low-carb, multigrain bread, reduced-fat peanut butter, and sugar-free jelly.

Banana-Stuffed French Toast

Banana adds a delicious surprise to French toast.

PER SERVING: 210 cal., 4 g total fat (1 g sat. fat), 107 mg chol., 352 mg sodium, 34 g carb., 2 g fiber, 9 g pro. Exchanges: 1.5 starch, 0.5 carb., 0.5 medium-fat meat. Carb choices: 2.

Nonstick cooking spray
2 eggs or ½ cup refrigerated or frozen egg product, thawed
½ cup fat-free milk
½ teaspoon vanilla
⅛ teaspoon ground cinnamon
4 1-inch-thick slices French bread
⅔ cup thinly sliced banana
Sifted powdered sugar, light pancake and waffle syrup product, or maple syrup (optional)

1. Preheat the oven to 500°F. Line a baking sheet with foil; coat the foil with nonstick cooking spray. Set the baking sheet aside.

2. In a shallow bowl, combine eggs, milk, vanilla, and cinnamon. Beat with a wire whisk or rotary beater until mixed. Set aside.

3. Using a serrated knife, cut a pocket in each French bread slice, cutting horizontally from the top crust almost to, but not through, the bottom crust. Fill bread pockets with banana slices.

4. Dip the stuffed bread slices, one at a time, into egg mixture, coating both sides. Arrange the slices on the prepared baking sheet.

5. Bake slices, uncovered, for 10 to 12 minutes or until golden, turning once. If desired, sprinkle with powdered sugar or serve with syrup. Makes 4 (1-slice) servings.

Banana-Stuffed French Toast

(why bother with breakfast?)

There's no holiday from good nutrition! You already know that eating a healthful breakfast daily can help control your blood glucose. Here are three more reasons to start every day the right way.

1. Better performance. Breakfast eaters have a more positive attitude toward school and work, and they perform better. A Boston study showed that children who started eating breakfast raised their test scores significantly and were late or absent from school less frequently.

2. Better overall nutrition. People who eat breakfast are more likely to consume nutrients their bodies need. Skipping breakfast makes it hard to meet daily requirements for necessary nutrients.

3. Better weight control. Breakfast revs up your body's metabolic rate first thing in the morning, burning calories faster than if you skip it. Breakfast eaters maintain their weight more easily, too.

gathering for dinner

Mushroom-Sauced
Pork Chops

For your *family feast*, choose your bird by the number at your table— roast turkey for a big group or Cornish game hen for a *smaller gathering*. If pork is your pick, opt for Mustard-Maple Pork Roast or Mushroom-Sauced Pork Chops. Is fish more your kind of dish? Try salmon for your *holiday dinner*. Any meal you serve with such *good cheer* will make your holiday joyous!

Mushroom-Sauced Pork Chops

Mushroom soup and fresh mushrooms give a double dose of woodsy flavor.

PER SERVING: 314 cal., 12 g total fat (4 g sat. fat), 74 mg chol., 356 mg sodium, 17 g carb., 1 g fiber, 30 g pro. Exchanges: 0.5 vegetable, 1 carb., 4 very lean meat, 2 fat. Carb choices: 1.

- 4 pork loin chops, cut $\frac{3}{4}$ inch thick (about 2 pounds)
- 1 tablespoon cooking oil
- 1 small onion, thinly sliced
- 2 tablespoons quick-cooking tapioca
- 1 $10\frac{3}{4}$-ounce can reduced-fat and reduced-sodium condensed cream of mushroom soup
- $\frac{1}{2}$ cup apple juice or apple cider
- $1\frac{1}{2}$ teaspoons Worcestershire sauce
- 2 teaspoons snipped fresh thyme or $\frac{3}{4}$ teaspoon dried thyme, crushed
- $\frac{1}{4}$ teaspoon garlic powder
- $1\frac{1}{2}$ cups sliced fresh mushrooms
  Fresh thyme sprigs (optional)

1. Trim fat from chops. In a large skillet, heat oil over medium heat. Add chops; cook until brown, turning to brown evenly. Drain off fat.

2. In a $3\frac{1}{2}$- or 4-quart slow cooker,* layer onion and chops. Using a mortar and pestle, crush tapioca. In a medium bowl, combine tapioca, mushroom soup, apple juice, Worcestershire sauce, snipped thyme, and garlic powder; stir in mushrooms. Pour over chops.

3. Cover; cook on low-heat setting for 8 to 9 hours or on high heat for 4 to $4\frac{1}{2}$ hours. Serve sauce over chops. If desired, garnish with thyme. Makes 4 servings.

*Test Kitchen Tip: To use a 5- to 6-quart slow cooker, use 6 pork loin chops. Leave remaining ingredient amounts the same. Prepare as above. Makes 6 servings.

Mustard-Maple Pork Roast

Maple syrup, orange peel, and mustard add captivating flavor to the glaze for this succulent and impressive roast.

PER SERVING: 284 cal., 9 g total fat (3 g sat. fat), 62 mg chol., 303 mg sodium, 22 g carb., 3 g fiber, 28 g pro. Exchanges: 1/2 vegetable, 1 1/2 starch, 3 lean meat. Carb choices: 1.5.

- 1 2- to 2 1/2- pound boneless pork top loin roast (single loin)
- 2 tablespoons Dijon-style mustard
- 1 tablespoon sugar-free maple-flavored syrup
- 2 teaspoons dried sage, crushed
- 1 teaspoon finely shredded orange peel
- 1/4 teaspoon ground black pepper
- 1/8 teaspoon salt
- 20 to 24 tiny new potatoes, 1 1/2 to 2 inches in diameter (about 1 3/4 pounds)*
- 1 1-pound package peeled fresh baby carrots
- 1 tablespoon olive oil
- 1/4 teaspoon salt

1. Preheat oven to 325°F. Trim fat from roast. Place roast, fat side up, on a rack in a shallow roasting pan. In a small bowl, stir together mustard, syrup, sage, orange peel, pepper, and the 1/8 teaspoon salt. Spoon mixture onto roast, spreading evenly over the top. Insert an oven-going meat thermometer into center of roast. Roast for 30 minutes.

2. Meanwhile, peel a strip of skin from the center of each potato. In a 4-quart Dutch oven, cook potatoes, covered, in enough lightly salted boiling water to cover for 5 minutes. Add carrots; cook for 5 minutes more. Drain. Return to saucepan. Add olive oil and the 1/4 teaspoon salt; toss gently to coat.

3. Place potato mixture in roasting pan around roast. Roast for 45 minutes to 1 hour more or until meat thermometer registers 155°F. Remove roast from oven; cover tightly with foil. Let stand for 15 minutes before slicing. (The temperature of the meat after standing should be 160°F.) Makes 8 servings.

*Tip: If your potatoes are larger, use fewer potatoes to make 1 3/4 pounds. Cut any large potatoes in half.

Mustard-Maple Pork Roast

Chili-Glazed Pork Roast

For presentation and to control portions, plate the roast and vegetables in the kitchen.

PER SERVING: 134 cal., 4 g total fat (2 g sat. fat), 50 mg chol., 37 mg sodium, 2 g carb., 0 g fiber, 20 g pro. Exchanges: 3 very lean meat, 0.5 fat. Carb choices: 0.

- 1 tablespoon packed brown sugar
- 1 tablespoon snipped fresh thyme or 1 teaspoon dried thyme, crushed
- 1 teaspoon chili powder
- 1 teaspoon snipped fresh rosemary or 1/4 teaspoon dried rosemary, crushed
- 1/8 teaspoon cayenne pepper
- 1 2- to 2 1/2-pound boneless pork top loin roast (single loin)
   Fresh rosemary sprigs (optional)

1. Preheat oven to 325°F. In a small bowl, combine brown sugar, thyme, chili powder, snipped fresh rosemary, and cayenne pepper. Sprinkle sugar mixture evenly onto roast; rub in with your fingers.

2. Place pork roast on a rack in a shallow roasting pan. Insert an oven-going meat thermometer into center. Roast for 1 1/4 to 1 1/2 hours or until thermometer reads 155°F.

3. Cover roast with foil; let stand for 15 minutes. (The temperature of the meat after standing should be 160°F.) Slice before serving. If desired, garnish with rosemary sprigs. Makes 8 to 10 servings.

Make-Ahead Directions: Prepare roast as directed through Step 1. Cover and chill for up to 24 hours. Preheat oven to 325°F. Continue as directed in Step 2.

Seeded Pork Roast

A savory blend of seeds creates a crusty calorie-free coating. Apple juice lends a subtle sweetness.

PER SERVING: 220 cal., 9 g total fat (3 g sat. fat), 92 mg chol., 269 mg sodium, 5 g carb., 0 g fiber, 29 g pro. Exchanges: 4 lean meat. Carb choices: 0.5.

1	2½- to 3-pound (boneless) pork shoulder roast
1	tablespoon reduced-sodium soy sauce
2	teaspoons anise seeds, crushed
2	teaspoons fennel seeds, crushed
2	teaspoons caraway seeds, crushed
2	teaspoons dill seeds, crushed
2	teaspoons celery seeds, crushed
⅔	cup apple juice or apple cider
½	cup lower-sodium beef broth
1	tablespoon cornstarch

1. Trim fat from meat. If necessary, cut meat to fit into a 3½- to 5-quart slow cooker. Brush soy sauce onto meat. On a large piece of foil, combine anise seeds, fennel seeds, caraway seeds, dill seeds, and celery seeds. Roll roast in seeds to coat evenly. Place meat in slow cooker. Pour ⅓ cup of the apple juice and the broth around the meat.

2. Cover and cook on low-heat setting for 9 to 11 hours or on high-heat setting for 4½ to 5½ hours.

3. Transfer meat to a cutting board, reserving liquid. Slice meat; transfer to a platter. Cover to keep warm.

4. For gravy, strain cooking liquid; skim off fat. Transfer liquid to a small saucepan. In a small bowl, combine remaining ⅓ cup apple juice and cornstarch; stir into liquid in saucepan. Cook and stir over medium heat until thickened and bubbly. Cook and stir for 2 minutes more. Serve over meat. Makes 8 servings.

Pork Diane

Worcestershire sauce, Dijon mustard, and a double dose of lemon—lemon juice and lemon-pepper seasoning—add zest to this pork loin, perfect for a small gathering.

PER SERVING: 131 cal., 5 g total fat (2 g sat. fat), 55 mg chol., 377 mg sodium, 1 g carb., 0 g fiber, 19 g pro. Exchanges: 3 very lean meat, ½ fat. Carb choices: 0.

- 1 tablespoon **Worcestershire sauce for chicken**
- 1 teaspoon **lemon juice**
- 1 teaspoon **Dijon-style mustard**
- 4 **3-ounce boneless pork top loin chops, cut ¾ to 1 inch thick**
- ½ to 1 teaspoon **lemon-pepper seasoning**
- 1 tablespoon **butter or margarine**
- 1 tablespoon **snipped fresh chives, parsley, or oregano**

1. For sauce, in a small bowl, stir together 1 tablespoon *water,* Worcestershire sauce, lemon juice, and mustard; set aside.

2. Trim fat from chops. Sprinkle both sides of each chop with lemon-pepper seasoning. In a 10-inch skillet melt butter over medium heat. Add chops and cook for 8 to 12 minutes or until pork juices run clear (160°F), turning once halfway through cooking time. Remove from heat. Transfer pork chops to a platter; cover and keep warm.

3. Pour sauce into skillet; stir to scrape up any crusty browned bits from bottom of skillet. Serve sauce over chops. Sprinkle with chives. Makes 4 servings.

Pork Diane

Menu

Pork Diane *(opposite)*

Roasted Vegetable Couscous *(page 88)*

Light and Luscious Pumpkin Pie *(page 145)*

Roast Pork Loin Stuffed with Andouille and Crawfish

Andouille is a smoked pork sausage used in Cajun cooking.

PER SERVING: 305 cal., 11 g total fat (4 g sat. fat), 84 mg chol., 388 mg sodium, 9 g carb., 2 g fiber, 34 g pro. Exchanges: 0.5 starch, 4.5 meat. Carb choices: 0.5.

- 4 ounces (cooked) andouille or smoked turkey sausage, chopped
- 1 tablespoon olive oil
- 4 ounces fresh or frozen peeled crawfish tails, thawed
- 1 small onion, thinly sliced
- 1 stalk celery, thinly sliced
- 3 cups dried cubed whole wheat bread (about 5 slices)
- ¼ to ½ cup water
- 1 3½- to 4-pound boneless pork top loin roast (single loin)
- ¼ teaspoon ground black pepper
- 2 small white and/or red onions, cut into wedges
- 2 medium carrots, sliced
- 2 stalks celery, sliced ½ inch thick
- ½ cup bourbon or reduced-sodium beef broth
- 2 tablespoons tomato paste
- 4 cloves garlic, minced
- 2 cups reduced-sodium chicken broth
- 5 sprigs fresh thyme
- ½ sprig fresh rosemary

1. For stuffing, in a saucepan, cook sausage in hot oil for 2 minutes. Add crawfish, sliced onion, and celery; cook until tender. Add bread. Stir in water to moisten.

2. Preheat oven to 325°F. Trim fat from pork. Butterfly meat by making a lengthwise cut down the center to within ½ inch of other side; spread open. Starting in "V" of first cut, cut horizontally from center to ½ inch of other side. Repeat on opposite side; spread open. Cover with plastic wrap; pound pork until ½ inch thick (about a 15×9-inch rectangle).

3. Spread stuffing evenly onto pork, leaving 1 inch on each long side. Starting from a long side, roll into a spiral. Using 100-percent-cotton string, tie loin at even intervals until evenly shaped and tied. Sprinkle with pepper.

4. In a large roasting pan, combine onion wedges, carrots, and ½-inch celery slices; place a rack over the vegetables. Place roast on top of rack (tuck vegetables under the roast). Insert an oven-going meat thermometer into center of roast. Roast for 2 to 2½ hours or until thermometer registers 155°F.

5. Remove roast and vegetables from pan, reserving drippings. Cover; let stand for 10 to 15 minutes. (The temperature of roast after standing should be 160°F.)

6. Meanwhile, for sauce, stir bourbon into reserved drippings in pan, scraping to loosen browned bits. Transfer to a saucepan. Stir in tomato paste and garlic. Bring to boiling; reduce heat. Simmer, uncovered, for 3 to 4 minutes or until thickened, stirring constantly. Stir in broth, thyme, and rosemary. Bring to boiling; reduce heat. Simmer, uncovered, for 10 minutes. Discard thyme and rosemary. Cool slightly. Pour into a food processor; cover and process until nearly smooth.

7. To serve, cut meat into ½- to ¾-inch slices. Serve meat and vegetables with sauce. Makes 12 servings.

Roast Rack of Lamb

Roast Rack of Lamb

Dried lavender, rosemary, garlic, dried cranberries, and bread crumbs coat this celebratory lamb roast. Look for dried lavender at health food stores or online.

PER SERVING: 212 cal., 11 g total fat (3 g sat. fat), 36 mg chol., 255 mg sodium, 9 g carb., 1 g fiber, 11 g pro. Exchanges: 0.5 starch, 1.5 lean meat, 1 fat. Carb choices: 0.5.

- 2 1-pound French-style lamb rib roasts (each rack about 8×4×1½-inches, 8 ribs)
- 1 cup Merlot or other dry red wine
- 2 cloves garlic, minced
- 1 teaspoon freshly grated nutmeg or ½ teaspoon ground nutmeg
- 3 tablespoons olive oil
- 1 tablespoon butter
- 1 tablespoon snipped fresh rosemary
- 2 cups soft whole wheat bread crumbs
- 3 tablespoon dried cranberries
- 1 tablespoon dried lavender (optional)
- ½ teaspoon salt
- ½ teaspoon ground black pepper

1. Peel off the lamb's layer of fell (membrane) and fat, if present, down to silver skin. Place roast in a large resealable plastic bag in a shallow dish. Add wine, 1 clove garlic, and nutmeg. Seal bag. Marinate in refrigerator for 4 to 24 hours, turning bag occasionally.

2. In a medium skillet, heat 1 tablespoon of the oil and 1 tablespoon butter over medium heat. Add rosemary and remaining garlic; cook for 1 minute. Add crumbs; cook and stir 3 minutes. Remove from heat. Add cranberries, lavender (if desired), salt, and pepper. Stir in remaining oil.

3. Preheat oven to 450°F. Remove lamb from marinade, reserving marinade. Place lamb, bone side down, in a shallow roasting pan lined with foil. Pat crumb mixture evenly onto lamb. Pour reserved marinade into pan.

4. Roast, uncovered, for 25 to 30 minutes or until meat thermometer registers 140°F (medium rare) or 155°F (medium). To prevent overbrowning, cover loosely with foil for last 5 minutes of roasting. (If roast is thicker than above dimensions, increase roasting time by 10 to 15 minutes and cover sooner.) Let stand for 15 minutes. Makes 8 servings.

(love that lamb)

When buying lamb, use the color as the guide. The darker the color, the older the animal. The cuts most often found at the supermarket include leg of lamb, rack of lamb, chops, and loin. These cuts can be cooked by roasting, broiling, sautéing, or grilling. It's best to serve these cuts rare or medium rare. Chops from the shoulder are best cooked by braising to tenderize them. Less tender cuts of lamb, such as those from the shoulder, breast, or shank, are also best if marinated before cooking.

Roasted Leg of Lamb with Red Wine-Shallot Sauce

Add mixed vegetables to the pan the last hour of roasting.

PER SERVING: 232 cal., 7 g total fat (3 g sat. fat), 86 mg chol., 313 mg sodium, 8 g carb., 0 g fiber, 26 g pro. Exchanges: 0.5 starch, 3 lean meat. Carb choices. 0.5.

- 1 4-pound leg of lamb
- 1 teaspoon lemon-pepper seasoning
- 1 sprig fresh rosemary
- 6 cloves garlic, quartered lengthwise
- ½ cup thinly sliced shallots
- 2 tablespoons butter
- ¼ cup seedless red raspberry preserves
- 1½ cups dry red wine
- ½ teaspoon finely shredded lemon peel
- ½ teaspoon salt
- ⅛ teaspoon ground black pepper

1. Preheat oven to 325°F. Trim fat from meat. Using a small knife, cut ½-inch-wide pockets about 1 inch deep in the meat at 1-inch intervals. Place meat, fat side up, on a rack in a shallow roasting pan. Season with lemon-pepper seasoning. Pull small bunches of leaves from the rosemary sprig. Push slivers of garlic and rosemary leaves into the pockets in the meat. Insert a meat thermometer in thickest portion of meat.

2. Roast lamb, uncovered, for 2 to 2¼ hours or until meat thermometer registers 140°F for medium-rare doneness or 155°F for medium doneness. Cover and let stand 15 minutes before carving. (The meat's temperature will rise 5° during standing time.)

3. Meanwhile, for sauce, in a saucepan, cook shallots in 1 tablespoon of the butter over medium heat until tender. Stir in preserves until melted. Stir in wine. Bring to boiling. Boil gently, uncovered, for 15 minutes or until reduced to 1⅓ cups. Whisk in remaining 1 tablespoon butter. Remove from heat. Stir in lemon peel, salt, and pepper. Serve warm with lamb. Makes 10 to 12 servings.

Roasted Leg of Lamb with Red Wine-Shallot Sauce

Garlic Chicken with Sweet Potatoes

Garlic Chicken with Sweet Potatoes

Whole garlic cloves become mellow
and buttery soft when roasted.

PER SERVING: 393 cal., 12 g total fat (2 g sat. fat), 119 mg chol., 481 mg sodium, 30 g carb., 4 g fiber, 40 g pro. Exchanges: 2 starch, 4.5 lean meat. Carb choices: 2.

- **3** heads garlic
- **2** tablespoons olive oil
- **1½** tablespoons snipped fresh rosemary
- **1** teaspoon ground black pepper
- **½** teaspoon salt
- **1** 3- to 3½-pound whole roasting chicken
- **3** medium sweet potatoes (1½ to 1¾ pounds), peeled and cut into 1-inch pieces
- **1** large sweet onion (such as Vidalia, Maui, or Walla Walla), cut into wedges

1. Preheat oven to 375° F. Separate the cloves of garlic (you should have about 30 cloves) and peel. Mince 4 cloves. Set aside remaining garlic cloves.

2. In a small bowl, combine minced garlic with 1 tablespoon of the olive oil, 1 tablespoon of the rosemary, the pepper, and ¼ teaspoon of the salt. Rub minced garlic mixture onto chicken.

3. Place 6 garlic cloves into the cavity of the chicken. Tie legs to tail. Twist wing tips under back. Place on a rack in a shallow roasting pan. Insert oven-going meat thermometer into center of an inside thigh muscle. Do not allow thermometer tip to touch bone. Roast, uncovered, for 1½ to 1¾ hours or until drumsticks move easily in their sockets and meat thermometer registers 180°F.

4. Meanwhile, place sweet potatoes, onion wedges, remaining garlic cloves, ½ tablespoon of the rosemary, and ¼ teaspoon of the salt in a 13×9×2-inch baking pan. Drizzle vegetable mixture with remaining 1 tablespoon olive oil; toss to coat. Place in oven on a separate rack and roast, uncovered, for 50 to 60 minutes or until tender, stirring every 15 minutes.

5. Remove chicken from oven. Cover loosely with foil and let stand 15 minutes before carving. Serve chicken with vegetables. Carve chicken, discarding skin before serving. Makes 4 to 6 servings.

Tomato Pesto Chicken Rolls

You can make these rolls up to 24 hours ahead.
Prepare as directed through Step 3; cover and chill.

PER SERVING: 254 cal., 8 g total fat (2 g sat. fat), 79 mg chol., 326 mg sodium, 8 g carb., 1 g fiber, 36 g pro. Exchanges: 1 vegetable, 5 very lean meat, 1 fat. Carb choices: 0.5.

Nonstick cooking spray
- **6** skinless, boneless chicken breast halves (about 1½ pounds total)
- **⅛** teaspoon ground black pepper
- **½** of an 8-ounce tub fat-free cream cheese
- **2** tablespoons purchased dried tomato pesto
- **2** tablespoons olive oil
- **⅓** cup seasoned fine dry bread crumbs
- **1** pound fresh asparagus spears

1. Preheat oven to 400°F. Lightly coat a 9×9×2-inch baking pan and a shallow roasting pan with nonstick cooking spray; set aside.

2. Place each chicken breast half between 2 pieces of plastic wrap. Using the flat side of a meat mallet, pound each breast half until ¼ inch thick. Remove and discard the plastic wrap. Sprinkle chicken with pepper.

3. For filling, in a small bowl, stir together cream cheese and tomato pesto. Place 2 tablespoons of the filling in the center of each breast. Fold in sides and roll up. Secure rolls with wooden toothpicks. Brush chicken pieces, using 1 tablespoon of the oil; roll in crumbs.

4. Place chicken rolls, seam sides down, in the prepared baking pan. Bake, uncovered, for 10 minutes.

5. Meanwhile, snap off and discard woody bases from asparagus. If desired, scrape off scales. Toss asparagus with remaining 1 tablespoon oil; arrange in prepared roasting pan. Place in oven alongside chicken.

6. Bake, uncovered, for 15 to 20 minutes more or until asparagus is crisp-tender and the chicken is no longer pink (170°F). Makes 6 servings.

Rosemary Chicken

While your meal simmers in the slow cooker, you have time to decorate, shop, or just relax.

PER SERVING: 161 cal., 2 g total fat (0 g sat. fat), 66 mg chol., 126 mg sodium, 8 g carb., 2 g fiber, 28 g pro. Exchanges: 0.5 vegetable, 4 very lean meat. Carb choices: 0.5.

Nonstick cooking spray
1½ pounds skinless, boneless chicken breast halves or thighs
1 8- or 9-ounce package frozen artichoke hearts
12 cloves garlic, minced
½ cup chopped onion
½ cup reduced-sodium chicken broth
2 teaspoons dried rosemary, crushed
1 teaspoon finely shredded lemon peel
½ teaspoon ground black pepper
1 tablespoon cornstarch
1 tablespoon cold water
Lemon wedges (optional)

1. Coat an unheated large nonstick skillet with nonstick cooking spray. Preheat over medium heat. Brown chicken, half at a time, in hot skillet.

2. In a 3½- or 4-quart slow cooker, combine frozen artichoke hearts, garlic, and onion. In a small bowl, combine broth, rosemary, lemon peel, and pepper. Pour over vegetables in slow cooker. Add browned chicken; spoon some of the garlic mixture over chicken.

3. Cover and cook on low-heat setting for 6 to 7 hours or on high-heat setting for 3 to 3½ hours.

4. Transfer chicken and artichokes to a platter, reserving cooking liquid. Cover chicken and artichokes with foil to keep warm.

5. If using low-heat setting, turn to high-heat setting. In a small bowl, combine cornstarch and the cold water. Stir into liquid in slow cooker. Cover and cook about 15 minutes more or until slightly thickened. Spoon sauce over chicken and artichokes. If desired, serve with lemon wedges. Makes 6 servings.

Menu

Lemon Chicken *(below)*

Spanish Rice with Pigeon Peas *(page 92)*

Green beans with almonds

Cranberry-Walnut Whole Wheat Rolls *(page 106)*

Lemon Chicken

The bread-crumb coating thickens the sauce.

PER SERVING: 254 cal., 8 g total fat (2 g sat. fat), 66 mg chol., 639 mg sodium, 15 g carb., 1 g fiber, 29 g pro. Exchanges: 1 starch, 3.5 very lean meat, 1.5 fat. Carb choice: 1.

4 skinless, boneless chicken breast halves (1 to 1¼ pounds)
¼ cup fat-free milk
⅔ cup fine dry bread crumbs
1 teaspoon adobo seasoning
2 tablespoons margarine or cooking oil
1¾ cups water
1 clove garlic, minced
1 lemon, halved crosswise
1 tablespoon snipped fresh parsley
Shredded lemon peel (optional)

1. Split chicken halves in half horizontally. Place milk in a shallow bowl. In a shallow dish, combine crumbs and adobo seasoning. Dip chicken into milk, then into crumb mixture, turning to coat evenly.

2. In a large nonstick skillet, cook chicken in hot margarine over medium heat about 5 minutes or until brown, turning occasionally.

3. Add the water and garlic. Squeeze juice from one lemon half onto chicken. Bring to boiling; reduce heat. Simmer, uncovered, about 15 minutes or until thickened, stirring often. Slice remaining lemon half.

4. To serve, top with parsley and, if desired, lemon peel. Serve with lemon slices. Makes 4 servings.

Lemon Chicken and Spanish Rice with Pigeon Peas

Feta-Stuffed Chicken Breasts

Feta-Stuffed Chicken Breasts

Cut into one of these juicy chicken pieces and you'll discover a festive feta cheese, tomato, and basil filling.

PER SERVING: 168 cal., 5 g total fat (2 g sat fat), 75 mg chol., 221 mg sodium, 1 g carb., 0 g fiber, 29 g pro. Exchanges: 4 very lean meat, 0.5 fat. Carb choices: 0.

- 1 tablespoon snipped dried tomatoes (not oil-packed)
- 4 skinless, boneless chicken breast halves (1 to 1½ pounds total)
- ¼ cup crumbled feta cheese (1 ounce)
- 2 tablespoons softened fat-free cream cheese (1 ounce)
- 2 teaspoons snipped fresh basil or ½ teaspoon dried basil, crushed
- ⅛ teaspoon ground black pepper
- 1 teaspoon olive oil or cooking oil
- Fresh basil sprigs (optional)

1. Place tomatoes in a small bowl. Pour enough boiling water over the tomatoes to cover. Let stand for 10 minutes. Drain and pat dry; set aside.

2. Meanwhile, using a sharp knife, cut a pocket in each chicken breast by cutting horizontally through the thickest portion to, but not through, the opposite side. Set aside.

3. In a small bowl, combine tomatoes, feta, cream cheese, and the snipped or dried basil. Spoon about 1 rounded tablespoon into each pocket. If necessary, secure openings with wooden toothpicks. Sprinkle chicken with pepper.

4. In a large nonstick skillet, cook chicken in hot oil over medium-high heat for 12 to 14 minutes or until tender and no longer pink, turning once (reduce heat to medium if chicken browns too quickly). Serve warm. If desired, garnish with basil sprigs. Makes 4 servings.

Moroccan Chicken

Serve this cumin-scented chicken on a bed
of couscous and chopped zucchini and carrot.

PER SERVING: 251 cal., 9 g total fat (2 g sat. fat), 92 mg chol., 121 mg sodium, 11 g carb., 0 g fiber, 30 g pro. Exchanges: 4 very lean meat, 1 carb., 1 fat. Carb choices: 1.

- 2 pounds meaty chicken pieces (breast halves, thighs, and drumsticks), skinned
- 2 teaspoons finely shredded orange peel (set aside)
- ½ cup orange juice
- 1 tablespoon olive oil
- 1 tablespoon grated fresh ginger
- 1 teaspoon paprika
- 1 teaspoon ground cumin
- ½ teaspoon ground coriander
- ¼ teaspoon crushed red pepper
- ⅛ teaspoon salt
- 2 tablespoons honey
- 2 teaspoons orange juice

1. Place the chicken pieces in a large resealable plastic bag set in a deep bowl. Set aside.

2. For marinade, in a small bowl, stir together the ½ cup orange juice, the olive oil, ginger, paprika, cumin, coriander, red pepper, and salt; pour over chicken. Seal bag; turn bag to coat chicken. Marinate in the refrigerator for 4 to 24 hours, turning bag occasionally.

3. Meanwhile, for glaze, in a small bowl, stir together orange peel, honey, and the 2 teaspoons orange juice.

4. Drain chicken, discarding the marinade. Preheat oven to 375°F. In a shallow baking dish, arrange the chicken, meaty sides up. Bake for 45 to 55 minutes or until chicken is done (170°F for breast halves; 180°F for thighs and drumsticks), brushing often with glaze the last 10 minutes of baking. Makes 4 servings.

Grilling Directions: Marinate chicken and prepare glaze as directed in Steps 1 through 3. Prepare grill for indirect grilling. Test for medium heat above pan. Arrange chicken pieces, meaty sides up, on lightly greased grill rack over drip pan. Cover and grill for 50 to 60 minutes or until chicken is done (170°F for breast halves; 180°F for thighs and drumsticks), brushing often with glaze the last 10 minutes of grilling.

Cornish Game Hen with Roasted Root Vegetables

Leave the peel on the potatoes and carrots for
a little extra fiber and a little less work.

PER SERVING: 345 cal., 12 g total fat (2 g sat. fat), 133 mg chol., 399 mg sodium, 27 g carb., 5 g fiber, 32 g pro. Exchanges: 1 vegetable, 1.5 starch, 3.5 lean meat. Carb choices: 1.5.

- 1 medium carrot, cut into large chunks
- 1 medium russet potato, cut into large chunks
- 1 medium parsnip or turnip, peeled and cut into chunks
- 1 small onion, cut into wedges
- 1 tablespoon olive oil
- 1 tablespoon balsamic vinegar
- 1 Cornish game hen or poussin (about 1½ pounds)
- 2 cloves garlic, minced
- 2 teaspoons snipped fresh rosemary or ½ teaspoon dried rosemary, crushed
- ¼ teaspoon salt
- ⅛ teaspoon ground black pepper

1. Preheat oven to 400°F. In a large bowl, combine carrot, potato, parsnip, and onion. Add oil and balsamic vinegar; toss gently to coat. Spread in a 9×9×2-inch baking pan; cover with foil. Roast for 30 minutes.

2. Meanwhile, gently separate the skin from the breast and the tops of drumsticks by slipping a paring knife or your fingers between the skin and meat to make 2 pockets that extend all the way to the neck cavity and the drumsticks.

3. In a small bowl, combine garlic, rosemary, salt, and pepper. Rub 2 teaspoons of the fresh rosemary mixture (or ½ teaspoon dried rosemary mixture) under skin onto breast and drumstick meat. Using 100-percent-cotton string, tie drumsticks to tail; tie wing tips to body. Rub remaining rosemary mixture onto the skin. If desired, insert a meat thermometer into the center of an inside thigh muscle, making sure it does not touch fat or bone.

4. Reduce oven temperature to 375°F. Stir vegetables. Place hen, breast side up, in baking pan with vegetables. Roast vegetables and hen, uncovered, for 1 to 1¼ hours or until vegetables are tender, hen juices run clear, and the thermometer registers 180°F, stirring vegetables once or twice during roasting.

5. Remove string from hen. Cover with foil; let stand for 10 minutes before serving. If desired, serve hen and vegetables on a platter with vegetables. To serve, use kitchen shears or a sharp knife to cut hen in half lengthwise; discard skin. Serve with vegetables. Makes 2 servings.

Turkey Piccata

(10 twists on citrus)

Add zest to holiday meals and snacks with these citrus ideas.

1. **Serve lycopene-rich** cara cara oranges and finely shredded lime peel with light vanilla yogurt for dessert.
2. **Showcase** the intense flavor of anthocyanin-rich blood oranges by tossing segments into salsas and chutneys.
3. **Add tangerine or tangelo** segments to tuna or spinach salads for contrasts in color and flavor. The vitamin C-rich citrus helps you absorb the iron from the spinach.
4. **Partner grapefruit** or pummelo segments with avocado and your favorite greens for a refreshing salad.
5. **Simmer kumquats** to make marmalade or a tangy sauce for meat, poultry, fish, or tofu.
6. **Squeeze fresh lemon** or lime juice into marinades.
7. **Substitute lemon or lime** juice for some or all of the salt in sauces and soups.
8. **Stir up a dressing** of lime or lemon juice, a bit of zest, and olive oil to brighten the flavors of salads, steamed vegetables, or grilled meat.
9. **Enjoy the pleasant taste** of fresh lemon, lime, or orange slices or wedges in a glass of water, lemonade, or tea.
10. **Grate lemon or lime zest** into soups or risotto for flavor.

Turkey Piccata

A piccata in Italy is usually pan-fried veal in a lemon sauce. We used lean turkey and less flour and oil.

PER SERVING: 148 cal., 3 g total fat (0 g sat. fat), 57 mg chol., 323 mg sodium, 5 g carb., 0 g fiber, 24 g pro. Exchanges: 3.5 very lean meat, 0.5 fat. Carb choices: 0.

- **1 turkey breast tenderloin (13 to 15 ounces)**
- **2 tablespoons all-purpose flour**
- **¼ teaspoon salt**
- **¼ teaspoon ground black pepper**
- **2 teaspoons olive oil**
- **1 cup reduced-sodium chicken broth**
- **2 teaspoons finely shredded lemon peel**
- **2 tablespoons lemon juice**
- **2 cloves garlic, minced**
- **½ teaspoon dry mustard**
- **¼ cup sliced green onions**
- **Lemon peel strips (optional)**
- **Sliced green onions (optional)**
- **Thin lemon slices (optional)**

1. Split turkey breast tenderloin in half horizontally; cut each half crosswise to make 4 portions. Place each portion between 2 pieces of plastic wrap. Lightly pound turkey to about ⅜-inch thickness. Remove plastic wrap. In a shallow dish, combine flour, ⅛ teaspoon of the salt, and pepper. Evenly coat turkey with flour mixture; shake off excess flour mixture.

2. In a large nonstick skillet, heat oil over medium-high heat. Add turkey; cook about 6 minutes or until brown, turning once to brown evenly. Add broth, peel, lemon juice, garlic, dry mustard, and remaining ⅛ teaspoon salt to skillet. Bring to boiling; reduce heat. Simmer, uncovered, about 10 minutes or until turkey is no longer pink and liquid is slightly reduced.

3. Add green onions. Cook for 2 minutes more. To serve, if desired, top turkey with lemon peel strips, additional green onions, and lemon slices. Serve with some of the cooking liquid. Makes 4 servings.

Stuffed Turkey Tenderloins

As guests savor these moist cayenne pepper-crusted turkey tenderloins, they'll delight in the tangy spinach-and-goat cheese filling tucked inside.

PER SERVING: 254 cal., 10 g fat (4 g sat. fat), 95 mg chol., 478 mg sodium, 1 g carb., 2 g fiber, 38 g pro. Exchanges: 5.5 very lean meat, 1.5 fat. Carb choices: 0.

- **4 10- to 12-ounce turkey breast tenderloins**
- **4 cups chopped fresh spinach leaves**
- **6 ounces semisoft goat cheese (chèvre) or feta cheese, crumbled (about 1½ cups)**
- **½ teaspoon ground black pepper**
- **2 tablespoons olive oil**
- **2 teaspoons paprika**
- **1 teaspoon salt**
- **¼ teaspoon cayenne pepper**

1. Make a pocket in each turkey breast tenderloin by cutting lengthwise from one side almost to, but not through, the opposite side; set aside.

2. In a large bowl, combine spinach, cheese, and black pepper. Spoon spinach mixture into pockets, dividing evenly. To hold in stuffing, tie 100-percent-cotton kitchen string around each tenderloin in 3 or 4 places.

3. In a small bowl, combine oil, paprika, salt, and cayenne pepper; brush evenly onto tenderloins. Wrap meat in plastic wrap. Refrigerate for 4 to 24 hours.

4. Preheat oven to 375°F. Unwrap turkey and place in a shallow roasting pan. Roast about 40 minutes or until done (170°F). Remove and discard strings; slice turkey tenderloins crosswise. Makes 8 servings.

Roast Herbed Turkey

If you choose to stuff the bird, the roasting time will increase. Roast the bird until the temperature of the stuffing reaches at least 165°F.

PER SERVING: 295 cal., 9 g total fat (3 g sat. fat), 172 mg chol., 165 mg sodium, 2 g carb., 0 g fiber, 48 g pro. Exchanges: 7 very lean meat, 1 fat. Carb choices: 0.

- **1 10- to 12-pound turkey**
- **3 tablespoons snipped fresh sage or 1 tablespoon dried sage, crushed**
- **½ teaspoon salt**
- **½ teaspoon ground black pepper**
- **1 recipe Spiced Sweet Potato Stuffing (optional) (see recipe, page 92)**
- **1 tablespoon olive oil**
- **1 orange**
- **1 tablespoon honey**
- **Oranges, halved (optional)**
- **Fresh sage leaves (optional)**

1. Rinse turkey cavity; pat dry with paper towels. Season the cavity with 1 tablespoon sage, salt, and pepper. If desired, lightly pack in Spiced Sweet Potato Stuffing.

2. Preheat oven to 325°F. Pull turkey's neck skin to back; fasten with a skewer. Tuck ends of drumsticks under band of skin across the tail. If the band of skin is not present, tie drumsticks securely to tail with 100-percent-cotton string. Twist wing tips under back.

3. Place turkey, breast side up, on a rack in a shallow roasting pan. Brush with olive oil. Insert an oven-going meat thermometer into the center of one of the inside thigh muscles. Roast for 2¾ to 3 hours or until meat thermometer registers 180°F and center of stuffing (if using) registers 165°F.

4. Halve and juice orange. In a small bowl, combine orange juice, honey, and remaining 2 tablespoons snipped sage. Brush onto turkey. Cover turkey with foil; let stand for 15 minutes before carving. If desired, garnish with orange halves and sage leaves. Makes 16 servings.

Menu

Herbed-Lemon Turkey with Wild Mushroom Gravy

Cheesy Cauliflower
(page 81)

Rice pilaf

Creamy Lime Mousse
(page 138)

Herbed-Lemon Turkey

A luscious dried cherry and sage mixture is nestled just beneath the skin of the turkey for a burst of flavor.

PER SERVING: 224 cal., 6 g fat (1 g sat. fat), 105 mg chol., 73 mg sodium, 4 g carb., 0 g fiber, 36 g pro. Exchanges: 5 very lean meat, 1 fat. Carb choices: 0.

- **½ cup dried cherries**
- **2 tablespoons olive oil**
- **1½ teaspoons snipped fresh sage or ½ teaspoon dried sage, crushed.**
- **1 4½- to 5-pound whole turkey breast (bone-in)**
- **1 lemon, quartered**
- **1 medium onion, quartered**
- **Wild Mushroom Gravy (optional) (see recipe, right)**

1. Preheat oven to 325°F. In a blender or food processor combine cherries, 1 tablespoon olive oil, and sage. Cover; blend or process just until cherries are finely chopped.

2. Slip your fingers between the skin and meat of turkey breast to loosen skin. Lift skin and, using a spatula, carefully spread cherry mixture directly onto breast. Place turkey on a rack in a shallow roasting pan. Place lemon and onion quarters underneath turkey on rack. Insert an oven-going thermometer into breast, make sure the thermometer does not touch the bone. Brush with remaining 1 tablespoon oil.

3. Roast turkey, uncovered, in preheated oven for 1½ to 2¼ hours or until thermometer registers 170°F, covering with foil the last 45 minutes of roasting to prevent overbrowning. Cover and let stand for 15 minutes before carving. Makes 12 servings.

Herbed-Lemon Turkey with Wild Mushroom Gravy

Wild Mushroom Gravy

This exotic mushroom gravy is a no-fat addition to your holiday meal.

PER SERVING: 40 cal., 0 g fat (0 g sat. fat), 0 mg chol., 103 mg sodium, 9 g carb., 1 g fiber, 1 g pro. Exchanges: 0.5 carb. Carb choices: 0.5.

Nonstick cooking spray
4 ounces shallots, peeled and coarsely chopped (about 1 cup)
1½ cups sliced fresh exotic mushrooms (such as oyster, shiitake, and/or crimini) or sliced fresh button mushrooms
1 14-ounce can reduced-sodium chicken broth
¼ cup all-purpose flour
2 teaspoons balsamic vinegar

1 teaspoon snipped fresh oregano or marjoram or ¼ teaspoon dried oregano or marjoram, crushed
Dash ground black pepper

1. Lightly coat an unheated medium saucepan with cooking spray. Add shallots; cook and stir over medium heat about 6 minutes or until shallots are tender and golden brown. Add mushrooms; cook for 4 minutes more.
2. Stir together ½ cup of the broth and the flour; add to saucepan. Add remaining broth, the balsamic vinegar, and dried herb, if using. Cook and stir until thickened and bubbly; cook and stir for 1 minute more. Stir in fresh herb, if using. Season with pepper. Serve with turkey. Makes 12 (3-tablespoon) servings.

Beef Braciole

Beef Braciole

Braciole (BRA-zhule) are stuffed beef rolls.

PER SERVING: 162 cal., 6 g total fat (2 g sat. fat), 148 mg chol., 359 mg sodium, 4 g carb., 1 g fiber, 21 g pro. Exchanges: 0.5 vegetable, 3 lean meat. Carb choices: 0.

Nonstick cooking spray
2 pounds boneless beef eye round roast
¼ teaspoon salt
¼ teaspoon ground black pepper
6 hard-cooked eggs, peeled and chopped
¼ cup grated Romano cheese
3 cloves garlic, minced
2 tablespoons snipped fresh parsley
1 tablespoon snipped fresh oregano or 1 teaspoon dried oregano, crushed
¼ teaspoon salt
¼ teaspoon ground black pepper
½ cup water
3 cups reduced-sodium pasta sauce or three 8-ounce cans no-salt-added tomato sauce plus 2 teaspoons dried Italian seasoning, crushed, and ¼ teaspoon salt

1. Coat a 3-quart rectangular baking dish with nonstick cooking spray; set aside.

2. Trim fat from beef. Cut meat crosswise into 12 slices, each about ½ inch thick. Place each slice between 2 pieces of plastic wrap. Working from the center to the edges, gently pound meat with the flat side of a meat mallet to about ⅛-inch thickness. Sprinkle meat with ¼ teaspoon salt and ¼ teaspoon pepper.

3. Preheat oven to 375°F. For filling, in a medium bowl, combine chopped eggs, Romano cheese, garlic, parsley, oregano, ¼ teaspoon salt, and ¼ teaspoon pepper.

4. Spoon a scant ¼ cup of the filling onto each beef slice. Roll up. Secure each beef roll-up with a wooden toothpick.

5. Pour the water into the prepared baking dish. Arrange beef roll-ups in the dish. Cover with foil. Bake about 1¼ hours or until beef is tender.

6. Meanwhile, in a medium saucepan, heat pasta sauce over medium heat. (Or in a medium saucepan, combine canned tomato sauce, Italian seasoning, and ¼ teaspoon salt; heat through over medium heat.)

7. For each serving, spoon warm sauce onto a dinner plate. Using a slotted spoon, transfer a beef roll-up to each plate. Drizzle with a little cooking liquid. Top with additional tomato sauce. Makes 12 servings.

Menu

Beef Braciole *(at right)*

Broccoli Rabe with Garlic *(page 87)*

Thyme-Roasted Parsnips and Carrots *(page 87)*

Potato Parker House Rolls *(page 119)*

Salmon with Rosemary

Roast the peppers and tomatoes to concentrate their sweetness in this colorful holiday pasta dish.

PER SERVING: 319 cal., 19 g total fat (3 g sat. fat), 66 mg chol., 219 mg sodium, 10 g carb., 2 g fiber, 24 g pro. Exchanges: 1.5 veg. 3 lean meat, 2 fat. Carb choices: 0.5.

- 1 pound fresh or frozen skinless salmon fillets, cut into 5 pieces
- 2 medium yellow and/or green sweet peppers, cut into 1-inch pieces
- 8 ounces cherry tomatoes, halved (1½ cups)
- 2 tablespoons olive oil
- 1 tablespoon snipped fresh rosemary or 1 teaspoon dried rosemary, crushed
- ¼ teaspoon ground black pepper
- 6 ounces dried whole grain pasta (such as linguine, fettuccine, or penne) (optional)
- 2 tablespoons dry white wine
- 2 tablespoons balsamic vinegar
- ⅓ cup snipped fresh basil

1. Thaw salmon, if frozen. Rinse salmon; pat dry with paper towels. Set aside. Preheat the oven to 425°F.

2. In a 15×10×1-inch baking pan, combine sweet pepper pieces and tomatoes. Drizzle with olive oil and sprinkle with half of the rosemary, ¼ teaspoon salt, and the black pepper. Toss to coat. Roast, uncovered, for 20 minutes.

3. Meanwhile, cook pasta according to package directions; drain and keep warm.

4. Remove pan from oven. Stir wine and balsamic vinegar into vegetable mixture. Add salmon pieces to pan and turn to coat with wine mixture. Return to oven and roast about 10 minutes more or until salmon flakes easily when tested with a fork.

5. To serve, if desired, divide pasta among 4 plates. Top pasta with vegetable mixture and sprinkle with basil. Place salmon on vegetables and sprinkle with remaining rosemary. Makes 5 servings.

Salmon with
Whole Wheat Pasta

Salmon with Asparagus and Mushrooms

(fish for thought)

Serving fish for special occasions adds healthful variety to your menus. Not only does it taste good, but fish is a good source of high-quality protein and good-for-you fats. The fat in fish is mostly polyunsaturated and monounsaturated, unlike the saturated fat found in meat. Fish also has omega-3, ployunsaturated fatty acids thought to be beneficial in reducing blood clots, lowering LDL "bad" blood cholesterol levels, and reducing the risk of heart disease. Fish that are especially high in omega-3 fatty acids include sardine, herring, mackerel, Atlantic bluefish, tuna, salmon, pilchard, butterfish, and pompano.

Salmon with Asparagus and Mushrooms

Very few foods naturally contain vitamin D. The salmon and mushrooms in this recipe give you a double dose.

PER SERVING: 371 cal., 20 g total fat (4 g sat. fat), 67 mg chol., 289 mg sodium, 12 g carb., 3 g fiber, 28 g pro. Exchanges: 1.5 vegetable, 0.5 carb., 3.5 lean meat, 2.5 fat. Carb choices: 1.

- 4 fresh or frozen skinless salmon fillets, cut about 1 inch thick (about 1 pound total)
- ¼ teaspoon kosher salt
  Ground black pepper
- 2 tablespoons olive oil
- 2 cups sliced assorted fresh mushrooms (such as button, cremini, and/or stemmed shiitake)
- 1 cup chopped onion
- 6 cloves garlic, minced (1 tablespoon)
- 1 tablespoon chopped fresh thyme or dried thyme, crushed
- 1 cup dry white wine
- 1 cup clam juice, fish stock, chicken stock, or reduced-sodium chicken broth
- 2 cups 1½-inch-long pieces of asparagus
- 1 cup cherry tomatoes, halved
- 1 tablespoon chopped fresh flat-leaf parsley
- 1 teaspoon lemon juice
  Fresh thyme sprigs (optional)

1. Thaw fish, if frozen. Rinse fish; pat dry with paper towels. Measure thickness of fish fillets. Season fish with kosher salt and pepper. Set aside.

2. In a large skillet, heat 1 tablespoon of the olive oil over medium heat. Add mushrooms; cook about 5 minutes or until golden. Add onion, garlic, and thyme; cook until mushrooms are tender, stirring occasionally. Add wine. Bring to boiling; reduce heat. Simmer, uncovered, about 15 minutes or until liquid is reduced to ¼ cup. Add clam juice. Return to boiling; reduce heat. Simmer, uncovered, 15 minutes more or until liquid is reduced to ¾ cup.

3. Add asparagus. Cover; cook about 3 minutes or until asparagus is crisp-tender. Stir in tomatoes, parsley, and lemon juice. Season to taste with kosher salt and pepper. Transfer to a platter and keep warm.

4. In the same skillet, heat remaining 1 tablespoon olive oil over medium heat. Add salmon; cook for 4 to 6 minutes per ½-inch thickness of salmon or until salmon flakes easily when tested with a fork, turning once. Serve salmon over vegetable mixture. If desired, garnish with fresh thyme. Makes 4 servings.

Basil-Buttered Salmon

Use the leftover basil-and-butter mixture to season your favorite cooked vegetables.

PER SERVING: 294 cal., 19 g total fat (5 g sat. fat), 94 mg chol., 113 mg sodium, 0 g carb., 0 g fiber, 28 g pro. Exchanges: 4 lean meat, 1.5 fat. Carb choices: 0.

- 4 fresh or frozen skinless salmon, halibut, or sea bass fillets, cut about 1 inch thick (about 1¼ pounds)
- ½ teaspoon salt-free lemon-pepper seasoning
- 2 tablespoons butter, softened
- 1 teaspoon snipped fresh lemon basil, regular basil, or dill or ¼ teaspoon dried basil or dill weed, crushed
- 1 teaspoon snipped fresh parsley or cilantro
- ¼ teaspoon finely shredded lemon peel or lime peel

1. Thaw fish, if frozen. Rinse fish; pat dry with paper towels. Sprinkle with lemon-pepper seasoning.

2. Place fish on the greased unheated rack of a broiler pan. Turn any thin portions under to make uniform thickness. Broil 4 inches from the heat for 5 minutes. Carefully turn fish over. Broil for 3 to 7 minutes more or until fish flakes easily when tested with a fork.

3. Meanwhile, in a small bowl, stir together butter, basil, parsley, and lemon peel. To serve, spoon 1 teaspoon of the butter mixture onto each fish piece. Cover and refrigerate remaining butter mixture for another use. Makes 4 servings.

Grilling Directions: Place fish on the greased rack of an uncovered grill directly over medium coals. Grill for 8 to 12 minutes or until fish flakes easily when tested with a fork, carefully turning once halfway through grilling.

Basil-Buttered Salmon

Spice-Rubbed Salmon with Tropical Rice

Salmon is one of the richest sources of heart-healthy omega-3 fatty acids.

PER SERVING: 366 cal., 13 g total fat (3 g sat. fat), 66 mg chol., 155 mg sodium, 35 g carb., 3 g fiber, 26 g pro. Exchanges: 0.5 fruit, 2 starch, 3 lean meat. Carb choices: 2.

PER SERVING WITH SUBSTITUTE: same as above, except 353 cal., 154 mg sodium, 32 g carb.

1 1-pound fresh or frozen skinless salmon fillet
 Nonstick cooking spray
1 tablespoon coriander seeds, coarsely crushed*
1 tablespoon packed brown sugar or brown sugar substitute** equivalent to 1 tablespoon brown sugar
1 teaspoon lemon-pepper seasoning
1 recipe Tropical Rice (see right)
 Lemon wedges (optional)
 Fresh cilantro (optional)

1. Thaw salmon, if frozen. Spray a shallow baking pan with nonstick cooking spray. Preheat oven to 450°F. Rinse salmon; pat dry with paper towels. Measure the thickness of the salmon. Place salmon in the prepared pan.

2. In a small bowl, stir together coriander seeds, brown sugar, and lemon-pepper seasoning. Sprinkle fish with mixture; using fingers press seasoning slightly.

3. Bake fish for 4 to 6 minutes per ½-inch thickness or until it flakes easily when tested with a fork.

4. Serve salmon with Tropical Rice. If desired, garnish with lemon wedges and fresh cilantro. Makes 4 servings (1 piece of salmon plus ½ cup rice).

Tropical Rice: In a medium bowl, stir together 2 cups hot cooked brown rice; 1 seeded, peeled, and chopped mango; 1 tablespoon snipped fresh cilantro; and 1 teaspoon finely shredded lemon peel. Serve warm.

***Test Kitchen Tip:** If you don't have coriander seeds to crush for the fish coating, substitute 1 tablespoon sesame seeds (toasted, if desired) and ¼ teaspoon ground cumin.

****Sugar Substitutes:** Choose from Sweet'N Low Brown or Sugar Twin Granulated Brown. Follow the package directions to use the product amount that's equivalent to 1 tablespoon brown sugar.

Pecan-Crusted Fish with Peppers and Squash

Pecans and cornmeal combine for a satisfying crunch that makes this fish stand out from any fried variety. Serve it with the colorful vegetables that bake alongside the fish.

PER SERVING: 358 cal., 18 g total fat (3 g sat. fat), 53 mg chol., 481 mg sodium, 26 g carb., 4 g fiber, 24 g pro. Exchanges: 1.5 vegetable, 1 starch, 2.5 very lean meat, 3 fat. Carb choices: 2.

1 pound fresh or frozen skinless catfish fillets, white fish, or orange roughy, cut ½ inch thick
 Nonstick cooking spray
½ cup yellow cornmeal
⅓ cup finely chopped pecans
½ teaspoon salt
¼ cup all-purpose flour
¼ teaspoon cayenne pepper
¼ cup refrigerated or frozen egg product, thawed, or 1 egg
1 tablespoon water
2 small red and/or orange sweet peppers, seeded and cut into wedges
1 medium zucchini, bias-sliced ½ inch thick
1 medium yellow summer squash, bias-sliced ½ inch thick
2 teaspoons cooking oil
¼ teaspoon seasoned salt
 Lemon wedges (optional)

Spice-Rubbed Salmon with Tropical Rice

Pecan-Crusted Fish with Peppers and Squash

1. Preheat oven to 425°F. Thaw fish, if frozen. Rinse fish; pat dry with paper towels. Cut fish into 3- to 4-inch pieces; set aside. Line a 15×10×1-inch baking pan with foil. Coat foil with cooking spray; set aside.

2. In a shallow dish, stir together cornmeal, pecans, and salt. In another dish, stir together flour and cayenne. In a small bowl, whisk egg and water. Dip each fish piece into flour mixture, shaking off excess. Dip fish into egg mixture, then into pecan mixture. Place in prepared pan.

3. In a large bowl, combine sweet peppers, zucchini, and squash. Add oil and seasoned salt; toss gently to coat. Arrange vegetables next to fish, overlapping as needed to fit.

4. Bake, uncovered, for 20 to 25 minutes or until fish flakes easily when tested with a fork and vegetables are crisp-tender. If desired, serve with lemon wedges. Makes 4 servings.

Menu

Provençal Fish Fillets
(at right)

Steamed green beans

Mixed greens salad

Whole wheat rolls

Provençal Fish Fillets

(cook fish right)

Minutes count when cooking fish. Weigh dressed fish or use a ruler to measure the thickness of the fillets and steaks in order to better estimate when to check for doneness. Properly cooked fish is opaque, flakes when tested with a fork, and readily comes away from the bones; the juices should be a milky white. Methods for cooking fish include baking, broiling, frying, microwaving, poaching, and grilling.

Provençal Fish Fillets

Cooks and their guests in Provence, France, have long benefited from heart-healthy olives, tomatoes, and fish.

PER SERVING: 161 cal., 5 g total fat (1 g sat. fat), 48 mg chol., 292 mg sodium, 7 g carb., 2 g fiber, 21 g pro. Exchanges: 1 vegetable, 3 very lean meat, 1 fat. Carb choices: 0.5.

- 4   4-ounce fresh or frozen skinless cod, catfish, pollock, or tilapia fillets, cut $\frac{1}{2}$ to 1 inch thick
- 1   tablespoon olive oil
- 1   medium onion, thinly sliced
- 2   cloves garlic, minced
- 1 $14\frac{1}{2}$-ounce can whole tomatoes, drained and chopped
- 8   oil-cured Greek olives, pitted and halved, or 8 pitted ripe olives, halved
- 2   teaspoons snipped fresh thyme or $\frac{1}{2}$ teaspoon dried thyme, crushed
- 1   teaspoon capers, drained
    Nonstick cooking spray
    Fresh thyme sprigs (optional)

1. Thaw fish, if frozen. Rinse fish under cold water; pat dry with paper towels. Measure thickness of fish. Set fish aside.

2. For sauce, in a small saucepan, heat oil over medium heat. Add onion and garlic; cook about 5 minutes or until tender, stirring occasionally. Add tomatoes, olives, the snipped or dried thyme, and capers. Heat to boiling; reduce heat to medium. Simmer, uncovered, about 10 minutes or until most of the liquid has evaporated.

3. Meanwhile, preheat broiler. Spray unheated rack of a broiler pan with cooking spray. Place fish on rack, tucking under any thin edges. Broil 3 to 4 inches from heat for 4 to 6 minutes per $\frac{1}{2}$-inch thickness or until fish flakes easily, turning once if fillets are 1 inch thick. Serve with sauce. If desired, garnish with fresh thyme sprigs. Makes 4 servings.

Ginger-Marinated Sea Bass

You'll love how easy sweet-spicy-salty marinade is to make for last-minute guests.

PER SERVING: 193 cal., 3 g total fat (1 g sat. fat), 69 mg chol., 556 mg sodium, 6 g carb., 0 g fiber, 33 g pro. Exchanges: 4 very lean meat, 1 carb. Carb choices: 0.5.

- 4   6-ounce fresh or frozen sea bass or halibut steaks, cut 1 inch thick
- $\frac{1}{4}$ cup light teriyaki sauce
- 2   tablespoons lemon juice
- 1   tablespoon grated fresh ginger
- 2   teaspoons brown sugar
- $\frac{1}{8}$ teaspoon cayenne pepper
- 2   cloves garlic, minced
    Nonstick cooking spray
    Fresh cilantro sprigs (optional)

1. Thaw fish, if frozen. Rinse fish; pat dry with paper towels. Place fish in a shallow nonmetallic dish. For marinade, in a small bowl, combine teriyaki sauce, lemon juice, ginger, brown sugar, cayenne pepper, and garlic. Pour onto fish; turn fish to coat. Cover and marinate in the refrigerator for 1 to 2 hours, turning fish occasionally. Drain fish, reserving marinade.

2. Coat the unheated rack of a broiler pan with cooking spray. Place fish on the prepared rack. Broil about 4 inches from the heat for 8 to 12 minutes or until fish flakes easily when tested with a fork, turning and brushing once with reserved marinade. Discard any remaining marinade. If desired, garnish with cilantro. Makes 4 servings.

Fish with Tangerine Relish

Here's an alternative to the traditional turkey with cranberry relish.

PER SERVING: 175 cal., 4 g total fat (1 g sat. fat), 36 mg chol., 161 mg sodium, 11 g carb., 1 g fiber, 24 g pro. Exchanges: 0.5 fruit, 3.5 very lean meat, 0.5 fat. Carb choices: 1.

- 6 4-ounce fresh or frozen skinless halibut, cod, sole, or other white fish fillets
- ¼ teaspoon salt
- ¼ teaspoon ground black pepper
- ⅓ cup orange juice
- ¼ cup finely chopped red onion or shallot
- 2 teaspoons white balsamic vinegar or balsamic vinegar
- 1 teaspoon snipped fresh tarragon or rosemary or ½ teaspoon dried tarragon or rosemary, crushed
- 1 teaspoon olive oil
- 1 clove garlic, minced
   Dash bottled hot pepper sauce
   Nonstick cooking spray
- 4 medium tangerines
- 2 tablespoons snipped fresh parsley
- 6 cups torn mixed salad greens (optional)

1. Thaw fish fillets, if frozen. Preheat broiler. Rinse fish; pat dry with paper towels. Sprinkle with salt and black pepper. Measure thickness of fish; set aside.

2. In a small saucepan, combine orange juice, onion, balsamic vinegar, tarragon, oil, garlic, and hot pepper sauce. Bring to boiling; reduce heat. Simmer, uncovered, for 5 to 6 minutes or until reduced to about ⅓ cup. Remove from heat. Remove 2 tablespoons of the liquid; set both mixtures aside.

3. Coat the unheated rack of a broiler pan with nonstick cooking spray. Place fish fillets on rack. Brush both sides of each fillet with the reserved 2 tablespoons liquid. Turn under any thin portions of fish to make uniform thickness. Broil 4 inches from the heat for 4 to 6 minutes per ½-inch thickness or until fish flakes easily with a fork.

4. Meanwhile, for tangerine relish, peel tangerines and separate into segments. Remove seeds and cut up tangerine segments into bite-size pieces. In a small bowl, combine tangerines, the remaining orange juice mixture, and the parsley.

5. To serve, place fish on greens, if using. Spoon tangerine relish onto fish. Makes 6 servings.

Catfish with Red Pepper Sauce

Catfish has a mild flavor and firm flesh. Grill or broil the fillets and serve with our vitamin C-loaded sauce.

PER SERVING: 234 cal., 16 g total fat (3 g sat. fat), 53 mg chol., 355 mg sodium, 5 g carb., 2 g fiber, 19 g pro. Exchanges: 0.5 vegetable, 2.5 lean meat, 1.5 fat. Carb choices: 0.

- 4 4-ounce fresh or frozen skinless catfish fillets, cut ½ to 1 inch thick
- 1 recipe Red Pepper Sauce (see below)
- 2 tablespoons red wine vinegar
- 1 tablespoon olive oil
- ¼ teaspoon dried rosemary, crushed
- ¼ teaspoon salt
- ⅛ teaspoon ground black pepper
   Nonstick cooking spray

1. Thaw fish, if frozen. Prepare Red Pepper Sauce. Preheat broiler.

2. Rinse fish; pat dry with paper towels. Measure thickness. In a small bowl, combine vinegar, olive oil, and rosemary. Brush both sides of fish fillets with vinegar mixture. Sprinkle fish with salt and black pepper.

3. Coat the unheated rack of a broiler pan with nonstick cooking spray. Place fish on rack, tucking under any thin edges. Broil 3 to 4 inches from heat for 4 to 6 minutes per ½-inch thickness or until fish flakes easily, turning once if fish is 1 inch thick. Serve with warm Red Pepper Sauce. Makes 4 servings.

Red Pepper Sauce: In a small saucepan, heat 1 tablespoon olive oil over medium heat. Add 1 cup chopped red sweet pepper; cook until tender, stirring occasionally. Stir in 2 peeled, seeded, and chopped tomatoes; 1 teaspoon vinegar; ¼ teaspoon salt; ¼ teaspoon garlic powder; and a dash cayenne pepper. Cook for 5 minutes more, stirring often. Transfer mixture to a food processor or blender. Cover and process until nearly smooth. Return to pan; cover and keep warm.

Grilling Directions: Spray a grill basket with nonstick cooking spray. Place fish in basket, tucking under any thin edges. Place basket on the rack of an uncovered grill directly over medium coals. Grill for 4 to 6 minutes per ½-inch thickness of fish or until fish flakes easily when tested with a fork, turning basket once if fillets are 1 inch thick.

Basil-Lemon Shrimp Linguine

Look for high-fiber or whole grain pasta for more fiber.

PER SERVING: 336 cal., 6 g total fat (1 g sat. fat), 172 mg chol., 463 mg sodium, 39 g carb., 4 g fiber, 31 g pro. Exchanges: 1 vegetable, 2 starch, 3 very lean meat, 1 fat. Carb choices: 2.5.

- 1 pound fresh or frozen large shrimp in shells
- 6 ounces dried linguine
- ¼ teaspoon salt
- 8 ounces fresh asparagus spears, trimmed and cut diagonally into 2-inch pieces
- Nonstick cooking spray
- 2 cloves garlic, minced
- 1 cup thin yellow, red, and/or green sweet pepper strips
- ¼ cup snipped fresh basil or 1 tablespoon dried basil, crushed
- 1 teaspoon finely shredded lemon peel
- ¼ teaspoon salt
- ¼ teaspoon ground black pepper
- ¼ cup sliced green onions
- 2 tablespoons lemon juice
- 1 tablespoon olive oil
- Lemon wedges (optional)

1. Thaw shrimp, if frozen. Peel shrimp; devein, leaving tails intact. Rinse well.

2. Cook pasta according to the package directions, except use ¼ teaspoon salt and add asparagus the last 3 minutes of cooking; drain.

3. Meanwhile, lightly coat a large nonstick skillet with cooking spray. Heat over medium heat. Add garlic; cook and stir for 15 seconds. Add pepper strips; cook and stir for 2 minutes or until crisp-tender. Add shrimp, dried basil (if using), lemon peel, remaining ¼ teaspoon salt, and pepper. Cook and stir for 3 minutes or until shrimp turn pink. Remove from heat.

4. Add shrimp mixture to pasta mixture. Add fresh basil (if using), green onions, lemon juice, and oil; toss gently to coat. If desired, serve with lemon wedges. Makes 4 (2-cup) servings.

Curried Shrimp

For a taste of Thailand, this trendy shrimp dish has a flavorful coconut milk sauce.

PER SERVING: 154 cal., 3 g total fat (1 g sat. fat), 129 mg chol., 284 mg sodium, 11 g carb., 2 g fiber, 19 g pro. Exchanges: 1 vegetable, 2.5 very lean meat, 0.5 fat. Carb choices: 1.

- 1 pound fresh or frozen large shrimp
- 1 teaspoon olive oil
- 1 cup chopped onion
- 1 tablespoon grated fresh ginger
- ½ teaspoon curry powder
- ½ teaspoon ground cumin
- ¼ teaspoon cayenne pepper
- 6 ounces fresh pea pods, trimmed and halved lengthwise (2 cups)
- ¼ cup orange juice
- 3 tablespoons unsweetened light coconut milk
- ¼ teaspoon salt
  Cooked whole wheat couscous (optional)*
- ½ cup snipped fresh cilantro

1. Thaw shrimp, if frozen. Peel and devein; rinse and pat dry. Set aside.

2. In a large nonstick skillet, heat olive oil over medium heat. Add onion; cook and stir about 5 minutes or until tender. Add ginger, curry powder, cumin, and cayenne pepper; cook and stir for 1 minute. Add shrimp and peas, stirring to coat with the spices. Cook and stir about 3 minutes or until shrimp are opaque. Stir in orange juice, coconut milk, and salt; heat through.

3. If desired, serve shrimp mixture with couscous. Top each serving with cilantro. Makes 4 servings.

To cook couscous: In a medium saucepan, bring 1½ cups water to boiling. Stir in 1 cup whole wheat couscous; cover and remove from heat. Let stand for 5 minutes.

Menu

Curried Shrimp *(at left)*

Couscous

Mixed fruit salad

Frozen low-fat yogurt

Soy-Lime Scallops with Leeks

This time-saving meal is great for an indoor grill.

PER SERVING: 130 cal., 1 g total fat (0 g sat. fat), 37 mg chol., 478 mg sodium, 9 g carb., 1 g fiber, 20 g pro. Exchanges: 0.5 carb., 2.5 very lean meat, 0.5 vegetable. Carb choices: 0.5.

- 1 pound fresh or frozen sea scallops
- ¼ cup reduced-sodium soy sauce
- ¼ cup rice vinegar
- 4 baby leeks
- 8 medium green scallions, red scallions, or green onions
- 1 medium lime, halved

1. Thaw scallops, if frozen. Rinse scallops; pat dry with paper towels. For marinade, in a small bowl, combine soy sauce and rice vinegar; set aside.

2. Trim root ends and green tops of leeks. Rinse leeks thoroughly to remove any grit.

3. Place leeks, scallops, and scallions in a resealable plastic bag set in a shallow dish. Add marinade to bag. Seal bag; turn to coat scallops and vegetables. Marinate in refrigerator for 30 minutes.

4. Remove scallops, leeks, and scallions from bag. Discard marinade. Place leeks, scallops, scallions, and lime halves (cut sides down) on the rack of an uncovered grill directly over medium heat. Grill for 8 to 10 minutes or until scallops are opaque, turning scallops and vegetables occasionally. Remove scallions from grill rack before they overbrown.

5. To serve, transfer leeks and scallions to 4 dinner plates. Top with scallops. Using grilling tongs, remove limes from grill; squeeze over scallops. Makes 4 servings.

Soy-Lime Scallops with Leeks

(so-called shellfish)

Although "shellfish" is used for saltwater and freshwater invertebrates, such as mollusks, crustaceans, and echinoderms, the term is actually is a misnomer because these invertebrates are not fish at all. Regardless, eating shellfish is a healthy alternative to eating meat because they are low in saturated fat and high in omega-3 fatty acids. Be careful not to overcook any type of fish (salmon, sea bass, haddock, etc.), mollusk (clam, mussel, oyster, eye winkles, and scallop), or crustacean (shrimp, prawn, lobster, crayfish, and crab), or they will become tough and chewy. Carefully follow the guidelines given for the recipes in this section based on the thickness of the fish or the color (for shrimp or scallops) to know when they are done.

family-favorite
sides & salads

Broccoli with Goat Cheese and Walnuts

At your holiday dinner, *everyone remembers* the turkey, but it's really the trimmings—the sides and salads—that *make the feast memorable.* Those are the dishes that *add tradition* to your feast, such as green bean casserole or cranberry salad. *They're all here,* along with some exciting *new sides,* too.

Broccoli with Goat Cheese and Walnuts

Dressed up with tangy buttermilk and a topping of tart chèvre and walnuts, this side dish promises bold flavor.

PER SERVING: 105 cal., 7 g total fat (2 g sat. fat), 4 mg chol., 212 mg sodium, 9 g carb., 3 g fiber, 5 g pro. Exchanges: 1.5 vegetable, 1.5 fat. Carb choices: 0.5.

- 1 pound broccoli, trimmed and cut into 1-inch pieces
- ½ cup buttermilk
- 1 tablespoon chopped fresh flat-leaf parsley
- 1 tablespoon Dijon-style mustard
- 2 teaspoons olive oil
- 1 teaspoon chopped fresh thyme or ½ teaspoon dried thyme, crushed
- 1 teaspoon red wine vinegar
- 1 clove garlic, minced (½ teaspoon minced)
- ¼ teaspoon kosher salt
- ⅛ teaspoon ground nutmeg
- ⅛ teaspoon ground black pepper
- ½ cup thinly sliced red onion
- ¼ cup coarsely chopped walnuts, toasted
- 1 ounce semisoft goat cheese (chèvre) or feta cheese, crumbled

1. In a covered large saucepan, cook broccoli in a small amount of lightly salted boiling water for 6 to 8 minutes or until crisp-tender. Drain and set aside.

2. In a large bowl, whisk together buttermilk, parsley, mustard, olive oil, thyme, red wine vinegar, garlic, kosher salt, nutmeg, and pepper. Add broccoli and red onion; stir gently to coat. Top with walnuts and goat cheese. Makes 6 (¾-cup) servings.

Make-Ahead Directions: Prepare as directed, except do not top with nuts and cheese. Cover and chill for up to 4 hours. To serve, top with walnuts and cheese.

Garlic-Herb Mushrooms

Serve these mushrooms solo as an appetizer
or as a side, tossed with cooked peas.

PER SERVING: 81 cal., 5 g total fat (1 g sat. fat), 0 mg chol., 118 mg sodium,
5 g carb., 2 g fiber, 5 g pro. Exchanges: 1 vegetable, 1 fat. Carb
choices: 0.5.

- **3** cloves garlic, minced
- **3** shallots, peeled and cut into thin wedges
- **2** tablespoons olive oil or cooking oil
- **1¼** pounds maitake, shiitake, oyster, or white button mushrooms, broken into clusters or sliced (about 8 cups)
- **¼** cup snipped fresh mixed herbs such as tarragon, rosemary, basil, oregano, and/or parsley
- **¼** teaspoon coarse salt or salt
- **¼** teaspoon cracked black pepper

1. In a large skillet, cook garlic and shallots in hot oil over medium-high heat for 2 minutes. Add maitake mushrooms. Cook, stirring gently occasionally, for 10 to 12 minutes or until tender. (Button and oyster mushrooms take 6 to 8 minutes; shiitake mushrooms take 4 minutes.) Stir in herbs, salt, and pepper. Makes 6 to 8 (½-cup) servings.

Quick Tip:

Research suggests that a group of vegetables called cruciferous vegetables contains a phytochemical which helps our bodies break down potential carcinogens. Some examples of cruciferous vegetables include cauliflower, brussels sprouts, and broccoli.

Braised Brussels Sprouts with Shallots

Cheesy Cauliflower

When oven and stovetop space are at a premium, here's a dish that lightens the load by cooking in a slow cooker.

PER SERVING: 68 cal., 5 g total fat (3 g sat. fat), 16 mg chol, 286 mg sodium, 2 g carb., 1 g fiber, 4 g pro. Exchanges: 1 vegetable, 1 fat. Carb choices: 0.

- 1 large head cauliflower (about 2½ pounds), broken into 8 pieces
- ¼ teaspoon salt
- ¼ teaspoon ground black pepper
- ⅔ vegetable broth
- ½ of an 8-ounce package reduced-fat cream cheese (Neufchâtel), cubed
- ½ teaspoon dried thyme, crushed
- ½ cup shredded reduced-fat cheddar cheese (2 ounces)

1. Place cauliflower in a 4- to 5-quart slow cooker. Sprinkle with salt and pepper. Add vegetable broth.

2. Cover and cook on low-heat setting for 3 to 4 hours or on high-heat setting for 1½ to 2 hours. Using a slotted spoon, transfer cauliflower to a bowl.

3. For sauce, add cream cheese and thyme to liquid in cooker; whisk until smooth. Spoon sauce over cauliflower. Sprinkle with cheddar cheese. Makes 8 (½-cup) servings.

Braised Brussels Sprouts with Shallots

Sautéed with shallots, these small cabbages are delicious. The key: Don't cook them to the mushy stage; they're done when they're soft.

PER SERVING: 87 cal., 7 g total fat (1 g sat. fat), 0 mg chol., 37 mg sodium, 6 g carb., 2 g fiber, 2 g pro. Exchanges: 1 vegetable, 1.5 fat. Carb choices: 0.5.

- 1 pint fresh Brussels sprouts
- 2 tablespoons olive oil or cooking oil
- 1 shallot, finely chopped
- 1 clove garlic, minced
- 2 tablespoons water
- ¼ teaspoon lemon juice
- ¼ teaspoon fine sea salt
- ¼ teaspoon ground black pepper

1. Trim stems and remove any wilted outer leaves from Brussels sprouts. Wash and cut Brussels sprouts in half lengthwise.

2. Drizzle the oil in a large nonstick skillet and swirl it around until the oil coats the entire surface. Heat over high heat until hot. Reduce heat to medium and add shallot and garlic. Cook and stir until tender.

3. Add Brussels sprouts to skillet; toss to coat with hot oil. Add the water. Reduce heat to medium. Cover and cook for 7 to 8 minutes or until sprouts are soft.

4. Remove saucepan from heat. Sprinkle sprouts with lemon juice, salt, and pepper; toss to coat. Makes 4 (½-cup) servings.

Fresh Green Bean and Mushroom Casserole

A toasty whole grain topper replaces the traditional fried onion rings to keep fat and sodium in check.

PER SERVING: 107 cal., 3 g total fat (1 g sat. fat), 7 mg chol., 148 mg sodium, 14 g carb., 3 g fiber, 4 g pro. Exchanges: 1.5 vegetable, 0.5 carb., 0.5 fat. Carb choices: 1.

- 1½ pounds fresh green beans, trimmed
- 2 tablespoons butter or margarine
- 3 tablespoons all-purpose flour
- 1 tablespoon ranch dry salad dressing mix
- ¼ teaspoon ground white pepper
- 1½ cups fat-free milk
  Nonstick cooking spray
- 1 cup chopped onion
- 2 cloves garlic, minced
- 1½ cups sliced fresh mushrooms
- 1 cup soft whole wheat or white bread crumbs

1. Preheat oven to 375°F. In a covered large saucepan, cook green beans in a small amount of boiling water for 10 to 15 minutes or until crisp-tender.

2. Meanwhile, for white sauce, in a medium saucepan, melt butter. Stir in flour, dressing mix, and white pepper until combined. Stir in milk. Cook and stir over medium heat until thickened and bubbly; remove from heat.

3. Coat an unheated medium nonstick skillet with nonstick cooking spray. Preheat skillet over medium heat. Add onion and garlic; cook for 2 to 3 minutes or until tender.

4. Remove half of the onion mixture from skillet; set aside. Add mushrooms to remaining onion mixture in skillet; cook about 5 minutes or until tender.

5. Drain beans. In a 1½-quart casserole, combine beans, mushroom mixture, and white sauce.

6. For topping, in a small bowl, stir together reserved onion mixture and bread crumbs; sprinkle onto bean mixture. Bake, uncovered, for 25 to 30 minutes or until heated through. Makes 10 (½-cup) servings.

Fresh Green Bean and Mushroom Casserole

Root Vegetables with Hazelnuts

Hazelnuts add a satisfying crunch and interesting flavor to this easy dish.

PER SERVING: 77 cal., 4 g total fat (0 g sat. fat), 0 mg chol., 62 mg sodium, 10 g carb., 3 g fiber, 2 g pro. Exchanges: 2 vegetable, 0.5 fat. Carb choices: 0.5.

- 4 cups assorted peeled root vegetables (such as parsnips, turnips, and/or rutabaga) cut into 1-inch pieces
- 1 cup baby carrots, peeled (if desired)
- 1 cup pearl onions, peeled
- ½ cup peeled celeriac (celery root) cut into ¾-inch pieces
- ⅛ teaspoon salt
- ⅛ teaspoon ground white pepper
- 1 tablespoon olive oil
- ⅓ cup chopped hazelnuts (filberts), toasted

1. In a large saucepan, cover and cook root vegetables, carrots, pearl onions, and celeriac in a small amount of boiling water about 5 minutes or until vegetables are nearly tender. Drain.

2. In a large skillet, cook vegetables, salt, and pepper in hot olive oil for 8 to 10 minutes or just until tender, stirring occasionally. To serve, sprinkle with nuts. Makes 10 (¾-cup) servings.

(side dish savvy)

Look for ways to make everyday side dishes worthy of a holiday celebration. Search for ways to add herbs or interesting seasonings that will lend a flavorful nuance to your favorite vegetable dishes. Or add a new salad to your meal. Crisp, light, and refreshing, a tossed salad cleanses the palate and supplies vitamins and nutrients to your plate. Plus, research has shown that when you start a meal with a side salad, you're likely to eat fewer calories than you would for a meal without salad. To top off either your vegetable or salad, a toasty sprinkling of nuts—such as sliced almonds, walnuts, or pecans—adds crunch and a heart-healthy benefit as well.

**Root Vegetables
with Hazelnuts**

Southern Succotash

Haricots verts are just thin French green beans.

PER SERVING: 72 cal., 1 g total fat (1 g sat. fat), 3 mg chol., 23 mg sodium, 13 g carb., 3 g fiber, 3 g pro. Exchanges: 1 starch. Carb choices: 1.

- **1** 10-ounce package frozen lima beans
- **2½** cups French green beans (haricots verts) or green beans, trimmed
- **2** cups fresh or frozen whole kernel corn
- **1** tablespoon butter
- **½** to 1 teaspoon cracked black pepper

1. In a covered large saucepan, cook lima beans in boiling water for 10 minutes. Add green beans; cook for 5 minutes.

2. Add corn to the beans; cook for 5 minutes more. Drain vegetables. Stir in butter and pepper; toss gently to mix. Serve warm. Makes 12 (½-cup) servings.

Southern Succotash

Balsamic Roasted Carrots

A lively blend of brown sugar, molasses, and balsamic vinegar lends a subtle sweetness to make the carrots company special.

PER SERVING: 114 cal., 3 g total fat (2 g sat. fat), 8 mg chol., 179 mg sodium, 21 g carb., 4 g fiber, 2 g pro. Exchanges: 0.5 carb., 2 vegetable, 0.5 fat. Carb choices: 1.5.

- **4** pounds carrots, bias-cut into 2-inch pieces*
- **4** ounces shallots (3 large), cut into ½-inch-thick wedges
- **3** tablespoons butter
- **2** tablespoons packed brown sugar
- **1** tablespoon mild-flavor molasses
- **⅓** cup balsamic vinegar
- **½** teaspoon salt
  Fresh herb sprigs (optional)

1. Preheat oven to 450°F. Place carrots and shallots in a 13×9×2-inch baking pan; set aside.

2. In a large skillet, melt 2 tablespoons of the butter; heat until light brown. Stir in brown sugar, molasses, and balsamic vinegar; bring to boiling, stirring constantly. Boil gently, uncovered, for 2 minutes.

3. Pour balsamic vinegar mixture over carrots and shallots; toss. Roast, uncovered, for 50 to 60 minutes or until carrots are crisp-tender, stirring twice. Stir in remaining 1 tablespoon butter and the salt. Serve warm. If desired, garnish with fresh herb sprigs. Makes 12 (½-cup) servings.

*Note: If carrots are very thick, halve or quarter the thick end pieces after cutting into 2-inch chunks.

Make-Ahead Directions: Prepare as directed. Transfer to a storage container. Cover and refrigerate for up to 24 hours. (Carrots will darken and soften slightly.) Place carrot mixture in a 2-quart microwave-safe casserole. Cover and microwave on 100 percent (high) power for 7 to 8 minutes or until heated through, stirring once.

Braised Parsnips, Squash, and Cranberries

Acorn squash wedges make edible serving bowls.

PER SERVING: 164 cal., 3 g total fat (2 g sat. fat), 0 mg chol., 204 mg sodium, 35 g carb., 6 g fiber, 3 g pro. Exchanges: 2 starch. Carb choices: 2.

- 1 medium acorn squash, halved, seeded, and cut into 8 wedges
- 2 medium parsnips, peeled and cut into ½-inch slices (1¼ cups)
- 1 medium onion, cut into thin wedges
- 2 cloves garlic, minced
- 2 teaspoons olive oil or cooking oil
- ½ of a medium butternut squash, peeled and cut into 1-inch pieces
- ⅓ cup reduced-sodium chicken broth
- 1 teaspoon snipped fresh thyme or ¼ teaspoon dried thyme, crushed
- ¼ teaspoon salt
- ⅛ teaspoon ground black pepper
- ¼ cup dried cranberries
  Fresh thyme sprigs (optional)

1. Preheat oven to 450°F. On a large greased baking sheet, arrange acorn squash wedges, cut sides down. Roast about 20 minutes or until tender, turning once halfway through roasting time.

2. In a large skillet, cook parsnips, onion, and garlic in hot oil over medium heat for 3 minutes, stirring occasionally. Stir in butternut squash, chicken broth, snipped or dried thyme, salt, and pepper. Bring to boiling. Reduce heat; simmer, covered, over medium-low heat about 15 minutes or until vegetables are tender. Stir in cranberries. Cook 1 to 2 minutes more or until most of the liquid has evaporated.

3. Serve parsnip mixture over acorn wedges. If desired, garnish with thyme sprigs. Makes 4 servings.

Savory Pea Pods and Apples

Prep all but the apples ahead of time, then sauté this dish right before serving.

PER SERVING: 62 cal., 2 g total fat (0 g sat. fat), 3 mg chol., 92 mg sodium, 9 g carb., 2 g fiber, 2 g pro. Exchanges: 1.5 vegetable, 0.5 fat. Carb choices: 0.5.

- 3   slices turkey bacon, cut crosswise into thin strips
- 2   teaspoons olive oil
- 3   tart red cooking apples (such as Jonathan), cut into ½-inch-thick slices
- 2   medium leeks, chopped (⅔ cup)
- 4   cups fresh pea pods, trimmed
- ⅛   teaspoon salt
- ⅛   teaspoon ground black pepper

1. In a 12-inch skillet, cook turkey bacon in hot oil over medium heat for 2 to 3 minutes or just until crisp, stirring occasionally.

2. Add apples and leeks. Cook and stir for 3 to 4 minutes or just until apples are tender.

3. Add pea pods, salt, and pepper. Cover and cook for 2 to 3 minutes or until vegetables are crisp-tender. Makes 10 (½-cup) servings.

Cooked Peas and Celery

This quick-and-easy vegetable medley adds a light, garden-fresh note to any holiday meal.

PER SERVING: 75 cal., 2 g total fat (0 g sat. fat), 0 mg chol., 236 mg sodium, 11 g carb., 3 g fiber, 4 g pro. Exchanges: 1 starch. Carb choices: 1.

½ cup coarsely chopped red onion
1 tablespoon olive oil
½ cup sliced celery
2 10-ounce packages frozen peas
¼ cup chopped celery leaves (optional)
½ teaspoon salt
¼ teaspoon ground black pepper

1. In a large skillet, cook red onion in hot oil about 3 minutes or until softened. Stir in celery; cook about 2 minutes more or just until tender. Increase heat to medium-high; add peas. Cover and cook for 5 to 7 minutes more or until peas are heated through. Remove skillet from heat; stir in celery leaves (if desired), salt, and pepper. Makes 8 (½-cup) servings.

Broccoli Rabe with Garlic

Broccoli rabe may also be called broccoli di rape, raab, or rapini. Pictured on page 66.

PER SERVING: 48 cal., 3 g total fat (0 g sat. fat), 0 mg chol., 98 mg sodium, 4 g carb., 3 g fiber, 4 g pro. Exchanges: 1 vegetable, 0.5 fat. Carb choices: 0.

3 pounds broccoli rabe or 7 cups broccoli florets
2 tablespoons olive oil
6 cloves garlic, minced
¼ cup reduced-sodium chicken broth
½ teaspoon ground black pepper
¼ teaspoon salt

1. If using broccoli rabe, remove large leaves and, if necessary, cut stems to 6- to 8-inch-long pieces. In a 6- to 8-quart Dutch oven, cook broccoli, half at a time if necessary, in a large amount of boiling water, allowing 3 minutes for rabe or 6 minutes for florets. Drain well; gently squeeze to remove as much excess moisture as possible.

2. In the Dutch oven, heat oil over medium heat. Add garlic; cook and stir for 30 seconds. Carefully add broccoli (oil will spatter if broccoli is not drained well); cook and stir for 1 minute. Add broth; cook, uncovered, until evaporated, stirring often. Stir in pepper and salt. Serve warm. Makes 12 (½-cup) servings.

Thyme-Roasted Parsnips and Carrots

Roasting the carrots and parsnips gives them a slightly nutty flavor. Pictured on page 66.

PER SERVING: 70 cal., 2 g total fat (0 g sat. fat), 0 mg chol., 129 mg sodium, 12 g carb., 3 g fiber, 1 g pro. Exchanges: 1.5 vegetable, 0.5 fat. Carb choices: 1.

8 medium carrots, peeled and cut into bite-size pieces (4 cups)
2 to 3 medium parsnips, peeled and cut into bite-size pieces (4 cups)
2 tablespoons olive oil
1 tablespoon snipped fresh thyme or 1 teaspoon dried thyme, crushed
½ teaspoon salt
½ teaspoon ground black pepper

1. Preheat oven to 375°F. In a shallow roasting pan, combine carrots, parsnips, olive oil, thyme, salt, and pepper; toss to coat. Roast vegetables about 40 minutes or until tender and starting to brown, stirring occasionally. Makes 12 (½-cup) servings.

Dilled Peas and Mushrooms

Dill adds pizzazz to an otherwise humble dish.

PER SERVING: 78 cal., 2 g total fat (0 g sat. fat), 0 mg chol., 154 mg sodium, 11 g carb., 4 g fiber, 4 g pro. Exchanges: 0.5 vegetable, 0.5 starch, 0.5 fat. Carb choices: 1.

2 10-ounce packages frozen peas with pearl onions
1 small red sweet pepper, seeded and coarsely chopped (⅔ cup)
2 cups sliced fresh mushrooms
1 tablespoon olive oil
1 tablespoon snipped fresh dill or 1 teaspoon dried dill weed
¼ teaspoon salt
Dash black pepper

1. In a covered large saucepan, cook peas with pearl onions and sweet pepper in a small amount of boiling water about 5 minutes or until crisp-tender; drain well. Transfer to a medium bowl; set aside.

2. In the same saucepan, cook mushrooms in hot oil about 5 minutes or until tender, stirring occasionally. Stir in dill, salt, and pepper. Return mixture to saucepan; heat through. Makes 8 (½-cup) servings.

Herbed Corn Bread Dressing

Switch to a more healthful fat by using oil instead of butter in your favorite corn bread recipe or mix.

PER SERVING: 226 cal., 8 g total fat (1 g sat. fat), 18 mg chol., 492 mg sodium, 32 g carb., 3 g fiber, 7 g pro. Exchanges: 2 starch, 1.5 fat. Carb choices: 2.

Nonstick cooking spray
- 2   stalks celery, sliced
- ¾   cup chopped onion
- 2   cloves garlic, minced
- 2   tablespoons olive oil or cooking oil
- 4   cups crumbled corn bread
- 3   slices whole wheat bread, dried and crumbled
- ¼   cup snipped fresh parsley
- 1   tablespoon finely snipped fresh sage or 1½ teaspoons dried sage, crushed
- 2   teaspoons finely snipped fresh thyme 1 teaspoon dried thyme, crushed
- 1   teaspoon finely snipped fresh marjoram or ½ teaspoon dried marjoram, crushed
- ½   teaspoon ground black pepper
- ⅛   teaspoon salt
- ¾   cup refrigerated or frozen egg product, thawed, or 3 eggs, beaten
- ½   to ¾ cup reduced-sodium chicken broth

1. Preheat oven to 375°F. Lightly coat a 2-quart rectangular baking dish with cooking spray; set aside.

2. In a large skillet, cook celery, onion, and garlic in hot oil about 10 minutes or until tender.

3. In a very large bowl, combine corn bread and wheat bread. Add onion mixture, parsley, sage, thyme, marjoram, pepper, and salt; toss gently to mix.

4. Add egg; toss to coat. Add broth for desired moistness. Spoon into dish. Bake, uncovered, about 20 minutes or until hot in center (165°F). Makes 8 (⅔-cup) servings.

Roasted Vegetable Couscous

You can roast the vegetables ahead, if you like. Cover and chill them after roasting, then add to the cooked couscous and heat through.

PER SERVING: 141 cal., 3 g total fat (0 g sat. fat), 0 mg chol., 105 mg sodium, 25 g carb., 3 g fiber, 4 g pro. Exchanges: 1 vegetable, 1 starch, 0.5 fat. Carb choices: 1.5.

Nonstick cooking spray
- 1   Japanese eggplant or 1 small eggplant, halved lengthwise
- 1   small sweet onion (such as Walla Walla or Vidalia), halved
- 1   carrot, halved lengthwise
- 2   sweet pepper halves
- 1   or 2 yellow banana peppers, halved lengthwise and seeded
- ¾   cup quick-cooking couscous
- 1   recipe Balsamic-Mustard Dressing (see below)

1. Preheat oven to 375°F. Coat a shallow baking pan with cooking spray. Place vegetables, cut sides down, in the pan. Roast, uncovered, for 45 to 60 minutes or until tender. Wrap eggplant and peppers in foil; let stand for 20 minutes; peel. Cut vegetables into bite-size pieces.

2. Bring 1 cup water to boiling; stir in couscous. Remove from heat; let stand, covered, for 5 minutes.

3. In a bowl, combine vegetables, couscous, and Balsamic-Mustard Dressing; toss to coat. Makes 6 (⅔-cup) servings.

Balsamic-Mustard Dressing: In a screw-top jar, combine ¼ cup balsamic vinegar, 1 tablespoon salad oil, 1½ teaspoons Dijon-style mustard, ¼ teaspoon Nature's Seasoning blend, and ¼ teaspoon garlic powder. Cover; shake to mix.

(10 makeover tips)

Use these 10 strategies to cut fat and calories from your holiday dinner:

1. **Add more vegetables and fruit.** Serve a green salad with dinner, for example.
2. **Control portion sizes.** Keep an eye on how much you serve yourself.
3. **Switch to lower-fat dairy** foods. Even a small change from 2 percent to 1 percent will make a difference.
4. **Substitute olive oil** or trans-fat-free margarine for butter.
5. **Use low-calorie sweeteners** instead of sugar.
6. **Drink low-calorie** beverages.
7. **Cook brown rice** instead of white rice.
8. **Never say never.** Allow yourself a dessert or favorite food every now and then so you don't feel deprived.
9. **Choose whole grain** breads and rolls.
10. **Top potatoes** with yogurt instead of sour cream

Herbed **Corn Bread Dressing**

(veggie savvy)

Nonstarchy vegetables and legumes include artichokes, asparagus, beans (wax, Italian, and green), beets, broccoli, Brussels sprouts, cabbage, carrots, cauliflower, celery, cucumbers, eggplant, greens, mushrooms, onions, peppers, radishes, spinach, squash, tomatoes (which includes tomato sauce and juice), and zucchini. If you eat less than 1½ cups cooked or 3 cups raw of nonstarchy veggies at a meal, you don't have to count them in your daily meal plan. However, if you eat more than that, count it as a serving of starch.

Starchy vegetables and legumes include beans (baked, black, garbanzo, kidney, lima, pinto, Great Northern, navy or other dried beans), black-eyed or split peas, corn, lentils, mixed vegetables (with corn, peas, or pasta), plantains, sweet and white potatoes, winter squash, and yams. Starchy vegetables have the same amount of carbs as breads and cereals and can be used as the starch portion in the plate method (one-fourth of a 9-inch plate is dedicated to starch). Each portion (typically ½ cup) equals about 15 grams of carbohydrates.

Herbed Tomato Risotto Mix

Keep this mix in case you want a flavorful side dish fast.

PER SERVING OF RISOTTO: 80 cal., 0 g total fat (0 g sat. fat), 0 mg chol., 276 mg sodium, 17 g carb., 2 g fiber, 3 g pro. Exchanges: 1 starch. Carb choices: 1.

- 3¼ cups Arborio rice (two 12-ounce packages)
- ¾ cup thin strips dried tomatoes or snipped dried tomatoes (not oil-packed)
- 3 tablespoons dried minced onion
- 1 tablespoon dried Italian seasoning, crushed
- 1 teaspoon dried minced garlic

1. In a medium bowl, combine *uncooked* rice, dried tomatoes, dried minced onion, Italian seasoning, and dried minced garlic. Divide mixture among 8 small resealable plastic bags (about ½ cup mixture per bag). Seal and label. Store at room temperature for up to 3 months. Makes 8 bags dry mix (32 servings).

Herbed Tomato Risotto: In a heavy, medium saucepan, bring 1½ cups reduced-sodium chicken broth to boiling. Add 1 bag Herbed Tomato Risotto Mix. Return to boiling; reduce heat. Cover; simmer for 20 minutes, adding 1 cup desired frozen vegetables the last 5 minutes of cooking. Remove from heat. Let stand, covered, for 5 minutes or until rice is tender. If desired, stir in 2 tablespoons grated Parmesan cheese. Season with ground black pepper. If desired, sprinkle with snipped fresh basil. Makes 4 (½-cup) servings.

Herbed Tomato Risotto

Quick Tip:

Arborio is a short grain rice with a higher starch content than long grain or medium grain rices. This starchiness results in a creamier, stickier cooked rice, a much-loved characteristic of Italian risottos. Like other rices, Arborio is a member of the grass family.

Rosemary Roasted Potatoes and Tomatoes

Greek olives and olive oil, which browns and crisps the potatoes, add monounsaturated fat—better for heart health.

PER SERVING: 103 cal., 5 g total fat (1 g sat. fat), 2 mg chol., 208 mg sodium, 11 g carb., 2 g fiber, 3 g pro. Exchanges: 1 starch, 0.5 fat. Carb choices: 1.

- Nonstick cooking spray
- 1 pound tiny new potatoes, scrubbed and quartered (10 to 12)
- 2 tablespoons olive oil
- 1 teaspoon snipped fresh rosemary
- ¼ teaspoon salt
- ¼ teaspoon ground black pepper
- 4 plum tomatoes, quartered lengthwise
- ½ cup pitted kalamata olives, halved
- 3 cloves garlic, minced
- ¼ cup shaved Parmesan cheese (1 ounce)

1. Preheat oven to 450°F. Spray a 15×10×1-inch baking pan with nonstick cooking spray; place the potatoes in the pan.

2. In a small bowl, combine oil, rosemary, salt, and pepper; drizzle onto potatoes, tossing to coat. Bake for 20 minutes, stirring once.

3. Add tomato quarters, olives, and garlic; toss gently to coat. Bake for 5 to 10 minutes more or until potatoes are tender and brown on the edges and tomatoes are soft. Serve warm. Sprinkle with Parmesan cheese. Makes 8 (⅔-cup) servings.

Spanish Rice with Pigeon Peas

Pigeon peas are known as *gandules* in Hispanic shops. Pictured on page 59.

PER SERVING: 149 cal., 2 g total fat (0 g sat. fat), 0 mg chol., 307 mg sodium, 28 g carb., 3 g fiber, 5 g pro. Exchanges: 2 starch. Carb choices: 2.

- 2 cloves garlic, minced
- 1 tablespoon snipped fresh cilantro
- 1 teaspoon snipped fresh oregano or ¼ teaspoon dried oregano, crushed
- 1 teaspoon cooking oil
- 1¼ cups reduced-sodium chicken broth
- 1 tablespoon tomato paste
- 1 to 1½ teaspoons adobo sauce from canned chipotle chile peppers in adobo sauce
- ½ cup long grain white rice
- 1 cup canned pigeon peas or black-eyed peas, rinsed and drained

1. In a medium skillet, cook garlic, cilantro, and oregano in hot oil for 30 seconds.

2. Add broth, tomato paste, and adobo sauce; bring to boiling. Add *uncooked* rice; reduce heat. Cover; simmer 15 minutes or until tender, stirring once. Stir in peas; heat through. Makes 4 (about ½-cup) servings.

Spiced Sweet Potato Stuffing

Jamaican jerk spices give flavor to this stuffing.

PER SERVING: 89 cal., 1 g total fat (0 g sat. fat), 0 mg chol., 190 mg sodium, 18 g carb., 2 g fiber, 3 g pro. Exchanges: 1 starch. Carb choices: 1.

- ¾ reduced-sodium chicken broth
- 2 cups chopped, peeled sweet potatoes
- 12 slices raisin bread, lightly toasted and cubed (about 12 ounces)
- 2 teaspoons Jamaican jerk seasoning

1. Preheat oven to 325°F. In a medium saucepan, bring broth to boiling. Add sweet potatoes. Return to boiling; reduce heat. Cover and cook for 7 to 10 minutes or just until tender. Do not drain. Stir in raisin bread cubes and jerk seasoning until mixed. Add additional broth, if necessary, to moisten.

2. Spoon stuffing into a 1½-quart casserole. (Or prepare and bake stuffing as directed in Roast Herbed Turkey on page 64.) Cover and bake for 25 to 30 minutes or until heated through. Makes 12 (½-cup) servings.

Zucchini Bread Pudding

Serve this savory bread pudding instead of stuffing for a new twist to your holiday dinner menu.

PER SERVING: 191 cal., 7 g total fat (2 g sat. fat), 7 mg chol., 414 mg sodium, 22 g carb., 2 g fiber, 10 g pro. Exchanges: 1 starch, 1 very lean meat, 0.5 vegetable, 1 fat. Carb choices: 1.5.

- **Nonstick cooking spray**
- 2 medium zucchini, thinly sliced
- ½ cup fresh or frozen whole kernel corn
- 2 tablespoons olive oil
- ½ cup chopped bottled roasted red sweet peppers
- 1 tablespoon bottled minced garlic (6 cloves)
- 2 tablespoons snipped fresh basil or 2 teaspoons dried basil, crushed
- 1 tablespoon snipped fresh parsley or 1 teaspoon dried parsley flakes, crushed
- 1 tablespoon snipped fresh sage or 1 teaspoon dried sage, crushed
- 5 cups 1-inch sourdough or Italian bread cubes
- 1 cup shredded Italian cheese blend (4 ounces)
- ¼ cup chopped pecans
- 1¼ cups refrigerated or frozen egg product, thawed, or 5 eggs
- 2 cups fat-free milk
- ½ teaspoon salt
- ¼ teaspoon ground black pepper

1. Preheat oven to 350°F. Coat a 2-quart baking dish with nonstick cooking spray; set aside.

2. In a large skillet, cook and stir zucchini and corn in hot oil for 3 minutes. Stir in sweet peppers and garlic; cook and stir about 2 minutes more or until zucchini is tender. Stir in basil, parsley, and sage. Stir in the bread cubes.

3. Place half of the mixture in the prepared dish. Sprinkle with half of the cheese. Repeat the layers. Sprinkle with pecans.

4. In a bowl, beat egg slightly; whisk in milk, salt, and black pepper. Pour over bread mixture.

5. Bake, uncovered, about 35 minutes or until a knife inserted near center comes out clean. Let stand for 10 minutes. Serve warm. Makes 12 (⅔-cup) servings.

Make-Ahead Directions: Prepare as directed through Step 4. Cover and chill for up to 24 hours. Bake as directed in Step 5, except bake about 45 minutes.

Quick Tip:

Bread pudding is generally a sweet dessert made with eggs and cream. Savory versions have emerged, also using heavy dairy products. Pare down calories and fat in bread puddings by using milk instead of cream and egg product instead of eggs. Use whole grain breads to add fiber.

Zucchini Bread Pudding

Wilted Spinach with Olives

(6 valuable veggies)

Vegetables are usually low in calories and carbs, high in fiber, and loaded with vitamins and minerals. Use several for your healthful holiday meals.

1. **Carrots:** Bright orange carrots are loaded with carotenoids, which are good for eye health.

2. **Corn:** Fiber-rich corn contains the carotenoid beta-cryptoxanthin, which seems to protect lungs from cancer.

3. **Eggplant:** This source of potassium offers a fiber benefit, especially when cooked and eaten with the peel. The purple peel contains anthocyanin, an antioxidant that is said to protect from cancer.

4. **Green beans:** The high fiber content of beans, particularly the soluble fiber, can help keep blood glucose levels stable and might lower the risk of heart disease.

5. **Green onions and onions:** Quercetin, an antioxidant, might protect against some cancers. When consumed raw, onions might reduce the risk of diabetes and boost good HDL cholesterol.

6. **Spinach:** This leafy green is a good source of magnesium, a mineral that studies indicate might lower the risk of developing type 2 diabetes.

Kale Salad

Green Pepper Salad with Tangy Cayenne Dressing

If you enjoy fiery foods,
use the ½ teaspoon cayenne pepper.

PER SERVING: 55 cal., 3 g total fat (0 g sat. fat), 1 mg chol., 43 mg sodium, 7 g carb., 1 g fiber, 2 g pro. Exchanges: 1.5 vegetable, 0.5 fat. Carb choices: 0.5.

2 medium carrots, cut into thin bite-size strips
1 cup thin bite-size strips red, yellow, and/or green sweet pepper
½ of a small red onion, cut into strips
1 recipe Tangy Cayenne Dressing (see below)
10 cups torn mixed salad greens
⅓ cup chopped pecans, toasted

1. In a medium bowl, combine carrots, sweet pepper, and red onion; add Tangy Cayenne Dressing. Toss gently to coat. Serve over mixed greens. Sprinkle with pecans. Makes 12 (1-cup) servings.

Tangy Cayenne Dressing: In a large bowl, combine 1 cup vanilla low-fat yogurt, 2 minced cloves garlic, 1 tablespoon Worcestershire sauce, 1 teaspoon finely shredded lime peel, 1 tablespoon lime juice, and ¼ to ½ teaspoon cayenne pepper. Cover and chill for at least 2 hours.

Wilted Spinach with Olives

This salad might be easy, but the Mediterranean flavors will impress everyone at the table.

PER SERVING: 83 cal., 5 g total fat (2 g sat. fat), 12 mg chol., 392 mg sodium, 6 g carb., 4 g fiber, 5 g pro. Exchanges: 0.5 medium-fat meat, 1 vegetable, 0.5 fat. Carb choices: 0.5.

Nonstick cooking spray
3 tablespoons pitted kalamata olives (about 12)
8 cups lightly packed fresh spinach and/or mustard greens, stems removed
1 ounce feta cheese, crumbled

1. Coat an unheated large nonstick skillet with nonstick cooking spray. Preheat over medium heat. Add olives. Cook for 3 minutes, stirring often. Remove from skillet; set aside.

2. Increase heat to medium-high. Add spinach; cook 1 to 2 minutes or just until wilted, tossing often.

3. To serve, transfer spinach to a platter. Top with feta cheese and olives. Makes 2 (½-cup) servings.

Kale Salad

Down South, greens cooked with bacon are a soul-food staple. Ring in a new year/new you with fresh greens and a low-fat homemade salad dressing.

PER SERVING: 83 cal., 4 g total fat (1 g sat. fat), 0 mg chol., 243 mg sodium, 10 g carb., 3 g fiber, 3 g pro. Exchanges: 2 vegetable, 1 fat. Carb choices: 0.5.

3 cups finely chopped fresh kale
1 plum tomato, chopped
⅓ cup chopped red sweet pepper
¼ cup pitted ripe olives, quartered lengthwise
3 radishes, thinly sliced and halved
2 green onions, sliced
2 tablespoons sunflower kernels
¼ cup Zesty Lemon Dressing (see below)

1. In a large salad bowl, combine kale, tomato, sweet pepper, olives, radishes, onions, and sunflower kernels; toss gently. Top with Zesty Lemon Dressing; toss to coat. Makes 4 (1-cup) servings.

Zesty Lemon Dressing: In a screw-top jar, combine 3 tablespoons lemon juice, 3 tablespoons water, 2 tablespoons reduced-sodium soy sauce, 2 teaspoons olive oil, ½ teaspoon onion powder, and ¼ teaspoon garlic powder. Cover and shake well to mix. Chill until ready to serve or for up to 1 week. Makes ½ cup.

Apple Spinach Salad with Thyme-Dijon Vinaigrette

Pep up any salad with the leftover vinaigrette.

PER SERVING: 93 cal., 6 g total fat (1 g sat. fat), 0 mg chol., 96 mg sodium, 11 g carb., 2 g fiber, 1 g pro. Exchanges: 1 vegetable, 0.5 fruit, 1 fat. Carb choices: 1.

- **4** cups fresh baby spinach
- **1** medium green apple (such as Granny Smith), cored and sliced
- **¼** cup thin red onion wedges
- **2** tablespoons snipped dried tart red cherries
- **¼** cup Thyme-Dijon Vinaigrette (see right)
- **½** cup crumbled feta cheese or blue cheese (2 ounces) (optional)

1. In a large bowl, toss together spinach, apple, onion, and cherries. Shake Thyme-Dijon Vinaigrette; drizzle onto salad. Toss to coat. If desired, top each serving with cheese. Makes 4 (1-cup) servings.

Thyme-Dijon Vinaigrette: In a screw-top jar, combine ¼ cup olive oil, ¼ cup white or regular balsamic vinegar, 2 teaspoons snipped fresh thyme or ½ teaspoon crushed dried thyme, 1 teaspoon Dijon-style mustard, and ¼ teaspoon salt. Cover and shake well to mix. Chill until ready to serve. Makes ⅔ cup.

Make-Ahead Directions: Prepare the vinaigrette as directed. Cover and chill for up to 1 week.

Quick Tip:

Colorful beets brighten any holiday table for good reason. The beet itself is a good source of folate. Beet greens are high in vitamin A (beta-carotene) and vitamin C and are a good source of riboflavin and magnesium. Look for yellow, white, and striped red and white beets.

Hazelnut, Goat Cheese, and Tomato Salad with Chive Champagne Vinaigrette

If you prefer, use crumbled feta or blue cheese in place of the goat cheese.

PER SERVING: 107 cal., 10 g total fat (2 g sat. fat), 3 mg chol., 75 mg sodium, 3 g carb., 1 g fiber, 3 g pro. Exchanges: 1 vegetable, 2 fat. Carb choices: 0.

- 12 cups torn mixed salad greens (such as spinach, arugula, radicchio, and romaine)
- 2 medium tomatoes, cored and cut into wedges
- 3 ounces soft goat cheese (chèvre), crumbled
- ½ cup hazelnuts, toasted and chopped
- ½ cup Chive Champagne Vinaigrette (see below)

1. On a platter, arrange mixed greens, tomatoes, goat cheese, and hazelnuts. Drizzle with ½ cup Chive Champagne Vinaigrette. Cover and chill remaining dressing for other salads. Makes 12 (1-cup) servings.

Chive Champagne Vinaigrette: In a food processor, combine 2 finely chopped shallots, ⅓ cup champagne vinegar or white wine vinegar, 1 tablespoon lemon juice, ¼ teaspoon salt, and ¼ teaspoon ground black pepper. Cover and process until smooth. With the processor running, slowly add ½ cup olive oil in a steady stream. Stir in 2 tablespoons snipped fresh chives. Cover and chill. Before serving, let dressing stand at room temperature for 30 minutes. Stir before serving. Makes about 1 cup.

Make-Ahead Directions: Prepare Chive Champagne Vinaigrette as directed. Cover; chill for up to 5 days.

Beet Salad with Goat Cheese and Walnuts

Boost the nutty flavor by toasting the walnuts in the oven until golden.

PER SERVING: 147 cal., 10 g total fat (3 g sat. fat), 7 mg chol., 571 mg sodium, 11 g carb., 3 g fiber, 6 g pro. Exchanges: 0.5 medium-fat meat, 2.5 vegetable, 1.5 fat. Carb choices: 1.

- 2 small cooked beets or one 8¼-ounce can tiny whole beets, chilled
- 1 tablespoon snipped fresh basil or flat-leaf parsley
- ⅛ teaspoon ground black pepper
- 4 tablespoons bottled reduced-fat or fat-free balsamic vinaigrette salad dressing
- 4 cups mixed baby salad greens
- 2 tablespoons coarsely chopped walnuts, toasted
- 1 ounce soft goat cheese (chèvre), crumbled

1. Drain and cut up beets. In a medium bowl, combine cut-up beets, basil, and pepper. Drizzle with 2 tablespoons of the salad dressing; toss to coat.

2. Arrange greens on 2 salad plates; sprinkle with remaining dressing. Top with beet mixture, walnuts, and goat cheese. Makes 2 (1-cup) servings.

Beet Salad with Goat Cheese and Walnuts

(cook a batch of beans)

Canned beans are convenient timesavers in the kitchen. But if you worry about sodium, you might prefer to prepare your own dry beans for recipes. Cook up a batch and follow the directions for freezing them, below. Pull them from the freezer when you need them.

1. Cook a big batch of dried beans according to package directions until just tender.
2. Drain, cool, and place in freezer bags or containers in 1¾-cup portions (1¾ cups cooked beans equals a 15-ounce can of beans). Label; freeze the beans for up to three months.
3. To use, place the beans (thawed or frozen) in a saucepan with ½ cup water for each 1¾ cups of beans. Simmer, covered, over low heat until heated through. Drain and use.

**Black Bean Slaw
with Ginger Dressing**

Black Bean Slaw with Ginger Dressing

It might be winter, but you don't have to serve bleak salads! This flavorful slaw sings with freshness and color. Take advantage of purchased coleslaw mix to save time.

PER SERVING: 109 cal., 4 g total fat (1 g sat. fat), 0 mg chol, 289 mg sodium, 17 g carb., 5 g fiber, 5 g pro. Exchanges: 1 vegetable, 1 starch, 0.5 fat. Carb choices: 1.

- ½ of a 15-ounce can black beans, rinsed and drained
- 3 cups purchased shredded cabbage with carrot (coleslaw mix)
- 1 medium green apple, cored and chopped (⅔ cup)
- ½ cup chopped red sweet pepper
- 2 tablespoons cider vinegar
- 1 tablespoon reduced-sodium soy sauce
- 1 tablespoon peanut oil
- 1 teaspoon grated fresh ginger
- 1 teaspoon honey
- ⅛ teaspoon ground black pepper

1. In a large bowl, combine beans, coleslaw, apple, and sweet pepper.

2. For dressing, in a small screw-top jar, combine vinegar, soy sauce, peanut oil, ginger, honey, and black pepper; cover and shake well.

3. Pour dressing onto cabbage mixture; toss to coat. Cover and chill slaw for 1 to 24 hours. Makes 8 (1-cup) servings.

Radish and Garbanzo Bean Salad

Radish and Garbanzo Bean Salad

Winter radishes add crunch and holiday color.

PER SERVING: 115 cal., 4 g total fat (1 g sat. fat), 0 mg chol., 257 mg sodium, 16 g carb., 4 g fiber, 4 g pro. Exchanges: 0.5 starch, 2 vegetable, 0.5 fat. Carb choices: 1.

- **10 radishes, sliced**
- **3 medium tomatoes, chopped**
- **½ cup sliced green onions**
- **¼ cup chopped red onion**
- **1 15-ounce can garbanzo beans (chickpeas), rinsed and drained**
- **1 recipe Salad Vinaigrette (see below)**
- **8 cups torn mixed salad greens**
-   **Cracked black pepper (optional)**

1. In a large bowl, combine radishes, tomatoes, green onions, and red onion. Stir in beans.

2. Pour Salad Vinaigrette onto bean mixture; toss gently to coat. Cover and chill for 1 to 24 hours.

3. To serve, toss greens with bean mixture. If desired, top with pepper. Makes 8 (1¾-cup) servings.

Salad Vinaigrette: In a small bowl, whisk 2 tablespoons olive oil, 1 tablespoon white wine vinegar, and 1 teaspoon salad and vegetable seasoning mix.

Pecan-Cranberry Salad

Low-calorie gelatin thickens,
but doesn't set, this tangy take on traditional relish.

PER SERVING: 106 cal., 3 g total fat (0 g sat. fat), 0 mg chol., 27 mg sodium, 20 g carb., 2 g fiber, 1 g pro. Exchanges: 0.5 fruit, 1 carb., 0.5 fat. Carb choices: 1.

- 1 **12-ounce package fresh cranberries**
- 1 **cup water**
- ½ **cup sugar**
- 1 **4-serving-size package sugar-free cranberry- or raspberry-flavored gelatin**
- 1 **15¼-ounce can crushed pineapple (juice pack)**
- ⅓ **cup coarsely chopped pecans, toasted**

1. In a large saucepan, combine cranberries and the water. Bring to boiling; reduce heat. Simmer, uncovered, about 3 minutes or until berries pop.

2. Remove saucepan from heat. Add sugar and gelatin, stirring to dissolve. Stir in undrained pineapple. Transfer to a serving bowl. Cover and chill about 6 hours or until thick. Before serving, sprinkle with pecans. Makes 10 (⅓-cup) servings.

Quick Tip:

A few raw foods shouldn't be used in gelatin mixtures because they contain an enzyme that prevents the gelatin from setting up. These include fresh pineapple, kiwifruit, figs, guava, papaya, and gingerroot. After these foods have been cooked or canned, they can be used in gelatin.

Pear-Lime Salad

Pear-Lime Salad

Lime juice and peel lend a refreshing tang
to this creamy company-fancy salad mold.

PER SERVING: 82 cal., 1 g total fat (0 g sat. fat), 3 mg chol., 246 mg sodium, 12 g carb., 1 g fiber, 6 g pro. Exchanges: 0.5 fruit, 0.5 carb., 0.5 very lean meat. Carb choices: 1.

- 1 **16-ounce can pear halves (juice pack)**
- 1 **4-serving-size package sugar-free lime-flavored gelatin**
- ½ **cup boiling water**
- ½ **teaspoon finely shredded lime peel**
- 1 **tablespoon lime juice**
- 1 **8-ounce package fat-free cream cheese, softened**

1. Drain pears, reserving ⅔ cup juice. Chop pears; set aside.

2. In a bowl, combine gelatin and the boiling water; stir until gelatin is dissolved. Stir in reserved juice, the lime peel, and lime juice. Cover and chill about 45 minutes or until partially set (consistency of unbeaten egg whites).

3. In a bowl, beat cream cheese with an electric mixer on medium speed for 30 seconds; gradually beat in gelatin mixture. Fold in pears. Pour into a 3½- to 4-cup mold. Cover; chill about 4 hours or until set. To serve, unmold onto a platter. Makes 6 servings.

old-world breads

Chocolate-Cherry
Banana Bread

The tantalizing *aroma of bread* baking is a temptation that's hard to resist, especially when the breads have *holiday touches* from the old country. With these *multigrain and fruit specialties,* you don't have to pass on the bread basket, because you benefit so much from the fiber and the vitamins.

Chocolate-Cherry Banana Bread

Miniature chocolate pieces scatter throughout this quick bread, making a little chocolate seem like a lot.

PER SLICE: 119 cal., 2 g total fat (0 g sat. fat), 0 mg chol., 61 mg sodium, 23 g carb., 1 g fiber, 2 g pro. Exchanges: 0.5 starch, 1 carb., 0.5 fat. Carb choices: 1.5.
PER SLICE WITH SUBSTITUTE: same as above, except 108 cal., 19 g carb. Exchanges: 0.5 carb. Carb choices: 1.

Nonstick cooking spray
1½ cups all-purpose flour
⅔ cup sugar or sugar substitute blend* equivalent to ⅔ cup sugar
2 teaspoons baking powder
¼ teaspoon baking soda
¼ cup refrigerated or frozen egg product, thawed, or 1 egg
¼ cup fat-free dairy sour cream
¼ cup fat-free milk
2 teaspoons cooking oil
1 teaspoon vanilla
⅔ cup mashed banana (about 2 medium bananas)
8 maraschino cherries, drained and chopped
¼ cup chopped walnuts
2 tablespoons miniature semisweet chocolate pieces

1. Preheat oven to 350°F. Lightly coat the bottom of a 9×5×3-inch loaf pan with cooking spray; set aside.
2. In a bowl, stir together flour, sugar, baking powder, and baking soda. Make a well in center; set aside.
3. In a medium bowl, beat egg; stir in sour cream, milk, oil, and vanilla. Stir in banana; add to flour mixture. Stir just until moistened (batter should be lumpy). Fold in cherries, walnuts, and chocolate pieces.
4. Spoon batter into prepared pan. Bake for 35 to 40 minutes or until a toothpick inserted near the center comes out clean. Cool in pan on a rack for 10 minutes. Remove from pan. Cool on rack. Makes 1 loaf (16 slices).
*Sugar Substitutes: Choose from Splenda Sugar Blend for Baking or Equal Sugar Lite. Follow the package directions to use the amount equivalent to ⅔ cup sugar.

Orange-Date Pumpkin Bread

Orange-Date Pumpkin Bread

A loaf makes a delicious hostess gift.
Recommend serving with reduced-fat cream cheese flavored and a little grated orange peel stirred in.

PER SLICE: 129 cal., 4 g total fat (1 g sat. fat), 0 mg chol., 87 mg sodium, 22 g carb., 2 g fiber, 3 g pro. Exchanges: 0.5 starch, 1 carb., 0.5 fat. Carb choices: 1.5.

PER SLICE WITH SUBSTITUTE: same as above, except 120 cal., 20 g carb. Carb choices: 1.

Nonstick cooking spray
2 cups all-purpose flour
1⅓ cups whole wheat flour
2 teaspoons baking powder
1 teaspoon ground nutmeg
½ teaspoon salt
½ teaspoon baking soda
1 cup refrigerated or frozen egg product, thawed, or 4 eggs
1 15-ounce can pumpkin
¾ cup sugar or sugar substitute blend* equivalent to ¾ cup sugar
½ cup honey
⅓ cup cooking oil
1 teaspoon finely shredded orange peel
⅓ cup orange juice
½ cup chopped walnuts or pecans
½ cup snipped pitted dates or raisins

1. Preheat oven to 350°F. Coat the bottom and ½ inch up the sides of two 8×4×2-inch loaf pans with cooking spray; set aside.

2. In a large bowl, stir together all-purpose flour, whole wheat flour, baking powder, nutmeg, salt, and baking soda; set aside.

3. In a medium bowl, beat egg slightly; stir in pumpkin, sugar, honey, oil, orange peel, and orange juice.

4. Using a wooden spoon, stir pumpkin mixture into flour mixture just until combined. Stir in nuts and dates. Divide mixture between the prepared pans.

5. Bake about 50 minutes or until a wooden toothpick inserted near centers comes out clean.

6. Cool in pans on wire racks for 10 minutes. Remove from pans. Cool completely on wire racks. Makes 2 loaves (32 slices).

*Sugar Substitutes: Choose from Splenda Sugar Blend for Baking or Equal Sugar Lite. Follow the package directions to use the product amount equivalent ¾ cup sugar.

Date-Nut Bread

Be sure to purchase pitted whole dates rather than chopped dates, which are coated with sugar.

PER SLICE: 120 cal., 3 g total fat (1 g sat. fat), 13 mg chol., 172 mg sodium, 22 g carb., 3 g fiber, 3 g pro. Exchanges: 1 starch, 0.5 fruit. Carb choices: 1.5.

1 8-ounce package pitted whole dates, snipped
1 cup all-purpose flour
1 cup whole wheat flour
1 teaspoon baking soda
1 teaspoon baking powder
1 egg or ¼ cup refrigerated or frozen egg product, thawed
1 teaspoon vanilla
½ cup sliced almonds, toasted and coarsely chopped

1. In a medium bowl pour 1½ cups *boiling water* over dates. Let stand about 20 minutes or until dates are softened and mixture has cooled slightly.

2. Preheat oven to 350°F. Lightly grease bottom and ½ inch up sides of an 8×4×2-inch loaf pan; set aside. In a large bowl, stir together flours, baking soda, baking powder, and ½ teaspoon *salt*. In a small bowl, beat together egg and vanilla with a fork; stir into cooled date mixture. Add date mixture and almonds to flour mixture; stir until mixed. Spoon batter into pan, spreading evenly.

3. Bake for 50 to 55 minutes or until a toothpick inserted near the center comes out clean. Cool in pan on a wire rack for 10 minutes. Remove from pan. Cool completely on wire rack. Wrap in plastic wrap; store overnight before slicing. Makes 1 loaf (16 slices).

Spiced Fan Biscuits

These company-special biscuits taste so rich,
they need no spread.

PER BISCUIT: 121 cal., 4 g total fat (1 g sat. fat), 0 mg chol., 190 mg sodium,
18 g carb., 1 g fiber, 3 g pro. Exchanges: 1 starch, 1 fat. Carb choices: 1.

Nonstick cooking spray
2 cups all-purpose flour
4 teaspoons baking powder
½ teaspoon cream of tartar
¼ teaspoon salt
¼ cup shortening
¾ cup fat-free milk
2 tablespoons sugar
1 teaspoon ground cinnamon

1. Preheat oven to 450°F. Coat twelve 2½-inch muffin cups with nonstick cooking spray; set aside.

2. In a large bowl, stir together flour, baking powder, cream of tartar, and salt. Using a pastry blender, cut in shortening until mixture resembles coarse crumbs. Make a well in center; add milk. Stir just until the dough clings together.

3. Turn out dough onto a lightly floured surface. Knead by folding and gently pressing dough for 10 to 12 strokes or until dough is nearly smooth. Divide dough in half. Roll one half into a 12×10-inch rectangle.

4. In a small bowl, combine sugar and cinnamon. Sprinkle half of the sugar mixture onto rectangle.

5. Cut rectangle into five 12×2-inch strips. Stack strips; cut into six 2-inch-square stacks. Place each stack, cut side down, in a prepared muffin cup. Repeat with remaining dough and sugar mixture.

6. Bake for 10 to 12 minutes or until golden. Serve warm. Makes 12 biscuits.

Cranberry-Walnut Whole Wheat Rolls

Serve these crown-shaped rolls, studded with fruit and nuts, for dinner or breakfast.

PER ROLL: 119 cal., 3 g total fat (1 g sat. fat), 6 mg chol., 127 mg sodium, 19 g carb., 1 g fiber, 3 g pro. Exchanges: 1 starch, 0.5 fat. Carb choices: 1.

2¾ to 3¼ cups all-purpose flour
1 package active dry yeast
1 cup fat-free milk
¼ cup butter, margarine, or shortening
2 tablespoons sugar
1 teaspoon salt
½ cup refrigerated or frozen egg product, thawed, or 2 eggs
1¼ cups whole wheat flour
⅔ cup snipped dried cranberries
⅓ cup toasted and finely chopped walnuts or pecans
2 teaspoons finely shredded orange peel
Nonstick cooking spray

1. In a large mixing bowl, stir together 2 cups of the all-purpose flour and the yeast; set aside.

2. In a medium saucepan, heat and stir milk, butter, sugar, and salt just until warm (120°F to 130°F) and butter is almost melted.

3. Add warm mixture and egg to flour mixture. Beat with an electric mixer on medium for 30 seconds, scraping bowl. Beat on high for 3 minutes. Stir in whole wheat flour, cranberries, nuts, orange peel, and as much of the remaining all-purpose flour as you can.

4. Turn out onto a lightly floured surface. Knead in enough remaining all-purpose flour to make a moderately stiff dough that is smooth and elastic (6 to 8 minutes total). Shape into a ball. Place in a greased bowl; turn once to grease surface. Cover; let rise in a warm place until double in size (about 1 hour).

5. Punch dough down. Turn out onto a lightly floured surface. Divide dough in half. Cover; let rest for 10 minutes. Lightly coat twenty-four 2½-inch muffin cups with cooking spray; set aside.

Cranberry-Walnut Whole Wheat Rolls

6. To shape, divide each dough portion into 36 pieces. Shape each piece into a ball, pulling edges under to make smooth tops. Place 3 dough balls into each prepared muffin cup, smooth sides up. Cover and let rise in a warm place until nearly double in size (about 30 minutes).

7. Preheat oven to 375°F. Bake for 12 to 15 minutes or until golden. Remove rolls from muffin cups. Serve warm, or cool on wire racks. Makes 24 rolls.

Make-Ahead Directions: Prepare the dough as directed though Step 4, except do not let rise. Cover with greased plastic wrap; chill overnight or up to 24 hours. Let dough stand at room temperature for 30 minutes. Continue shaping as directed in Steps 5 through 7 (the rising in Step 6 may need an additional 10 to 15 minutes). You can also bake and freeze the rolls ahead of time and just reheat before serving.

Lefse

Serve half-rounds of this tender Norwegian flatbread.

PER SERVING: 95 cal., 3 g total fat (1 g sat. fat), 4 mg chol., 28 mg sodium, 14 g carb., 0 g fiber, 2 g pro. Exchanges: 1 starch, 0.5 fat. Carb choices: 1.
PER SERVING WITH SUBSTITUTE: same as above, except 90 cal., 13 g carb.

- 2 **cups all-purpose flour**
- 2 **tablespoons sugar or sugar substitute* equivalent to 2 tablespoons sugar**
- ⅛ **teaspoon salt**
- ½ **cup fat-free milk**
- ¼ **cup water**
- 3 **tablespoons shortening or canola oil****
- 2 **tablespoons butter, melted**
- 3 **tablespoons sugar**
- ¼ **teaspoon ground cinnamon**

1. In a large bowl, stir together flour, the 2 tablespoons sugar, and salt. In a small saucepan, heat and stir milk, the water, and shortening until warm (105°F to 115°F) and shortening (if using) is nearly melted. Pour onto flour mixture; stir until combined. Form into a ball. Cover dough with a wet, warm kitchen towel to keep slightly warm and moist while cooking lefse.

2. Pinch off about 3 tablespoons of the dough; shape into a ball. Dust ball lightly with flour; place on a well-floured surface. Using a well-floured lefse rolling pin, roll out dough ball into a circle about 8 inches in diameter (dough will be very thin). If necessary, lightly flour the top of the dough to prevent it from sticking to the rolling

Quick Tip:

Do you like the idea of using whole wheat flour but prefer the flavor of white flour? Why not give white whole wheat flour a try? It has a lighter flavor than whole wheat, has a finer grind, and can be used in most recipes as a 100 percent substitution for white flour.

pin. Using a lefse stick or large spatula, loosen the dough from the surface often, carefully pushing the stick between the dough and surface.

3. Heat an ungreased large flat griddle or large skillet over medium heat. (Or preheat a lefse grill.) Drape dough round over lefse stick or rolling pin and transfer it to the hot griddle. Cook lefse about 2 minutes or until light brown, turning about halfway through cooking (the top surface will be bubbly). Reduce heat, if necessary, to prevent overbrowning. (If the edges of lefse rounds begin to dry or curl, shorten cooking time. If the lefse rounds remain light in color, slightly increase cooking temperature.)

4. Place cooked lefse on a large kitchen towel. Cover with another towel. Repeat rolling and cooking remaining dough. Stack cooked lefse rounds; cover with kitchen towels to prevent drying.

5. To serve, brush one side of each lefse round very lightly with melted butter. In a small bowl, combine 3 tablespoons sugar and the cinnamon; sprinkle onto each lefse round. Roll up lefse rounds; cut in half. Makes 9 rounds (18 servings).

*Sugar Substitutes: Choose from Splenda granular, Equal Spoonful or packets, or Sweet'N Low bulk or packets. Follow package directions to use product amount equivalent to 2 tablespoons sugar.

**Test Kitchen Tip: If using canola oil, the dough will be quite sticky. Roll it out on a well-floured surface and use a floured rolling pin.

Make-Ahead Directions: Place stacked lefse in an airtight container; cover. Store in the refrigerator for up to 1 week or freeze for up to 3 months. Before serving, rinse each lefse lightly with warm water and place between kitchen towels; let stand for at least 15 minutes. When lefse rounds are soft, serve as directed in Step 5.

Wild Rice and Oat Bran Bread

Wild rice with its nutty flavor and chewy texture speckles this wholesome loaf.

PER SLICE: 120 cal., 2 g total fat (1 g sat. fat), 4 mg chol., 128 mg sodium, 22 g carb., 2 g fiber, 4 g pro. Exchanges: 1.5 starch. Carb choices: 1.5.

$1\frac{1}{4}$ to $1\frac{3}{4}$ cups bread flour
1 package active dry yeast
1 cup fat-free milk
2 tablespoons honey
2 tablespoons butter or shortening
$\frac{3}{4}$ teaspoon salt
1 cup whole wheat flour
$\frac{3}{4}$ cup cooked wild rice,* drained and cooled
$\frac{1}{3}$ cup oat bran
Nonstick cooking spray

1. In a large mixer bowl, stir together 1 cup of the bread flour and the yeast; set aside. In a medium saucepan, heat and stir milk, honey, butter, and salt just until warm (120°F to 130°F) and butter is almost melted. Add milk mixture to the flour mixture. Beat with an electric mixer on low speed for 30 seconds, scraping bowl constantly. Beat on high speed for 3 minutes. Using a wooden spoon, stir in whole wheat flour, wild rice, oat bran, and as much of remaining bread flour as you can.

2. Turn out dough onto a lightly floured surface. Knead in enough of the remaining bread flour to make a moderately stiff dough that is smooth and elastic (6 to 8 minutes total). Shape dough into a ball. Place in a lightly greased bowl; turn once to grease the surface. Cover and let rise in a warm place until double in size (1 to $1\frac{1}{4}$ hours).

3. Punch dough down. Turn out onto a lightly floured surface. Cover and let rest for 10 minutes. Coat an 8×4×2-inch loaf pan with cooking spray; set aside.

4. Shape dough into a loaf by patting or rolling. To shape by patting, gently pat and pinch dough into a loaf shape, tucking edges beneath. To shape by rolling, on a lightly floured surface, roll dough into a 12×8-inch rectangle. Roll up, starting from a short side. Seal seams with fingertips as you roll.

5. Place shaped dough in prepared pan. Cover; let rise in a warm place until nearly double in size (30 to 45 minutes). Preheat oven to 375°F.

6. Bake for 35 to 40 minutes or until bread sounds hollow when tapped. If necessary, cover loosely with foil the last 10 minutes to prevent overbrowning. Remove from pan. Cool on a wire rack. Makes 1 loaf (16 slices).

Bread Machine Directions: Add the ingredients to a $1\frac{1}{2}$-pound loaf bread machine according to the manufacturer's directions, except use $1\frac{3}{4}$ cups all-purpose flour and $1\frac{1}{4}$ teaspoons active dry yeast or bread machine yeast. If available, select the whole grain cycle or the basic white bread cycle. During the kneading cycle, check dough and, if necessary, add more bread flour or milk, 1 teaspoon at a time, to make a dough that forms a smooth ball. Remove hot bread from machine as soon as it is done. Cool on a wire rack.

*Test Kitchen Tip: For $\frac{3}{4}$ cup cooked wild rice, bring $\frac{3}{4}$ cup water and $\frac{1}{4}$ cup uncooked wild rice to boiling; reduce heat. Cover and simmer about 40 minutes or until wild rice is tender. Drain well.

Wild Rice and Oat Bran Bread

Four-Grain Bread

(10 whole grains)

Search out these grains for a new way to enjoy baked goods.

1. **Amaranth:** These tiny yellow to dark seeds cultivated by the Aztecs can be cooked or ground into flour.
2. **Brown rice:** Unpolished brown rice kernels may be ground into flour.
3. **Buckwheat:** You can buy buckwheat in the form of flour to make pancakes.
4. **Corn:** Use ground dried yellow or white cornmeal for baking corn bread, tamale pie, or cornmeal mush.
5. **Flax:** These small reddish brown seeds may be ground into flaxseed meal and used like flour. The seeds contain soluble fiber, which can help regulate blood glucose and lower blood cholesterol.
6. **Millet:** The oldest of cultivated grains, tiny unpolished whole millet kernels can be cooked whole or ground into millet flour.
7. **Quinoa:** These tiny South American seeds can be ground into flour.
8. **Rye:** Dark rye contains more bran than light rye and, therefore, more fiber.
9. **Wheat:** This grain is commonly ground into flour.
10. **Wild rice:** Not a true rice, this grain can be ground into flour.

Granary Bread

Millet lends a nutty, mildly sweet flavor to this bread. It contains high amounts of fiber, B vitamins, iron, and some vitamin E. Millet is thought to be one of the first cereal grains used for food.

PER SLICE: 125 cal., 1 g total fat (0 g sat. fat), 1 mg chol., 116 mg sodium, 24 g carb., 2 g fiber, 5 g pro. Exchanges: 1.5 starch. Carb choices: 1.5.

¼ cup bulgur
2 tablespoons millet
1¾ to 2¼ cups bread flour
1 tablespoon gluten flour (optional)
1 package active dry yeast
2 tablespoons molasses or honey
2 teaspoons butter or shortening
¾ teaspoon salt
1 cup whole wheat flour
¼ cup rolled oats
2 tablespoons toasted wheat germ
   Nonstick cooking spray

1. In a bowl, combine bulgur and millet. Add 1 cup *boiling water*. Let stand for 5 minutes; drain well.

2. In a large mixer bowl, stir together 1 cup of the bread flour, gluten flour (if using), and yeast; set aside.

3. In a saucepan, heat and stir 1¼ cups water, molasses, butter, and salt until warm (120°F to 130°F) and butter is almost melted. Add to flour mixture. Beat with an electric mixer on low for 30 seconds, scraping sides. Beat on high speed for 3 minutes. Stir in bulgur mixture, whole wheat flour, oats, wheat germ, and as much remaining bread flour as you can.

4. Turn out onto a lightly floured surface. Knead in enough of the remaining bread flour to make a moderately stiff dough that is smooth and elastic (6 to 8 minutes total). Shape into a ball. Place in a lightly greased bowl; turn once. Cover and let rise in a warm place until double in size (1 to 1¼ hours).

5. Punch dough down. Turn out onto a lightly floured surface. Cover; let rest for 10 minutes. Coat an 8×4×2-inch loaf pan with cooking spray; set aside.

6. Shape dough into a loaf; place loaf in prepared pan. Cover; let rise in a warm place until nearly double in size (about 30 minutes). Preheat oven to 375°F.

7. Bake for 35 to 40 minutes or until bread sounds hollow. Cover bread loosely with foil for the last 10 minutes to avoid overbrowning. Remove from pan. Cool on a wire rack. Makes 1 loaf (16 slices).

Four-Grain Bread

The fiber-rich four include oats, barley, whole wheat, and cornmeal. Freeze some loaves to bring out for company.

PER SLICE: 118 cal., 2 g total fat (0 g sat. fat), 0 mg chol., 183 mg sodium, 21 g carb., 2 g fiber, 4 g pro. Exchanges: 1.5 starch. Carb choices: 1.5.

⅓ cup quick-cooking rolled oats
⅓ cup quick-cooking barley
1¾ to 2¼ cups bread flour
½ cup whole wheat flour
1 package active dry yeast
1¼ cups warm water (120°F to 130°F)
2 tablespoons sugar
2 tablespoons cooking oil
⅓ cup cornmeal
   Nonstick cooking spray

1. Preheat oven to 375°F. Spread oats and barley in a shallow baking pan. Bake about 10 minutes or until light brown, stirring occasionally. Cool. Transfer mixture to blender. Cover; blend until ground. Set aside.

2. In a large mixer bowl, stir together 1 cup of the bread flour, the whole wheat flour, and yeast. Add warm water, sugar, oil, and 1¼ teaspoons *salt*. Beat with an electric mixer on low speed for 30 seconds, scraping bowl constantly. Beat on high speed for 3 minutes. Using a wooden spoon, stir in cornmeal, oat mixture, and as much of the remaining bread flour as you can.

3. Turn out dough onto a lightly floured surface. Knead in enough of remaining bread flour to make a moderately stiff dough that is smooth and elastic (6 to 8 minutes total). Shape into a ball. Place in a lightly greased bowl; turn once to grease the surface. Cover; let rise in a warm place until double in size (1 to 1¼ hours).

4. Punch dough down. Turn out onto a lightly floured surface. Cover; let rest for 10 minutes. Coat an 8×4×2-inch loaf pan with cooking spray; set aside. Shape dough into a loaf. Place in prepared pan. Cover; let rise in a warm place until nearly double (about 30 minutes).

5. Preheat oven to 375°F. Bake 40 minutes or until top is golden and bread sounds hollow when tapped. Remove from baking pan. Cool on a wire rack. Makes 1 loaf (16 slices).

Hearty Oat and Grain Bread

Hearty Oat and Grain Bread

Toasted and served with spreadable fruit or low-calorie preserves, this bread makes a simple breakfast special.

PER SLICE: 115 cal., 2 g total fat (0 g sat. fat), 0 mg chol., 124 mg sodium, 21 g carb., 3 g fiber, 4 g pro. Exchanges: 1.5 starch. Carb choices: 1.5.

⅓ cup cracked wheat
2 tablespoons cooking oil
2 tablespoons molasses
1 package active dry yeast
1 cup rolled oats
¼ cup nonfat dry milk powder
¼ cup oat bran or toasted wheat germ
1 teaspoon salt
1½ cups whole wheat flour
1½ to 2 cups all-purpose flour
1 tablespoon rolled oats
Nonstick cooking spray

1. In a small saucepan, bring 2 cups *water* to boiling; add cracked wheat. Reduce heat; cover and simmer for 5 minutes. Remove from heat; transfer to a large bowl. Stir in oil and molasses. Cool to lukewarm (105°F to 115°F). Add yeast; stir until dissolved. Add the 1 cup rolled oats, milk powder, oat bran, and salt.

2. Using a wooden spoon, stir in whole wheat flour; stir in as much of the all-purpose flour as you can. Turn out dough onto a lightly floured surface. Knead in enough of the remaining all-purpose flour to make a moderately stiff dough that is smooth and elastic (6 to 8 minutes total). Shape into a ball. Place in a lightly greased bowl; turn once to grease the surface. Cover and let rise in a warm place until double in size (about 1 hour).

3. Punch dough down. Cover; let rest for 10 minutes. Coat a baking sheet with cooking spray. Shape dough into an 8-inch round loaf; place on sheet. Cover; let rise in a warm place until nearly double (30 to 45 minutes).

4. Preheat oven to 375°F. Make 3 diagonal shallow slits across the top of the loaf. Brush lightly with *water*; sprinkle with the 1 tablespoon rolled oats.

5. Bake for 30 to 35 minutes or until loaf sounds hollow when tapped. Cool on rack. Makes 1 loaf (20 slices).

Seven-Grain Bread

This healthful loaf is full of robust wheat flavor—with a touch of honey for sweetness—and plenty of good-for-you grains, too.

PER SLICE: 111 cal., 2 g total fat (0 g sat. fat), 13 mg chol., 151 mg sodium, 20 g carb., 2 g fiber, 4 g pro. Exchanges: 1.5 starch. Carb choices: 1.5.

¾ to 1¼ cups all-purpose flour
½ cup seven-grain cereal
1 package active dry yeast
⅔ cup water
⅓ cup unsweetened applesauce
2 tablespoons honey
1 teaspoon salt
1 egg or ¼ cup refrigerated or frozen egg product, thawed
1¾ cups whole wheat flour
⅓ cup shelled sunflower kernels
Nonstick cooking spray

1. In a large mixing bowl, stir together ¾ cup of the all-purpose flour, the cereal, and yeast; set aside.

2. In a medium saucepan, combine the water, applesauce, honey, and salt; heat and stir just until warm (120°F to 130°F). Add applesauce mixture and egg to flour mixture. Beat with an electric mixer on low to medium speed for 30 seconds, scraping side of bowl constantly. Beat on high speed for 3 minutes. Using a wooden spoon, stir in the whole wheat flour, sunflower kernels, and as much of the remaining all-purpose flour as you can.

3. Turn out dough onto a lightly floured surface. Knead in enough of the remaining all-purpose flour to make a moderately stiff dough that is smooth and elastic (6 to 8 minutes total). Shape dough into a ball. Place in a lightly greased bowl; turn once to grease surface of dough. Cover; let rise in a warm place until double in size (1 to 1½ hours).

4. Punch dough down. Turn out onto a lightly floured surface; cover and let rest for 10 minutes. Coat an 8×4×2-inch loaf pan with cooking spray; set aside.

5. Shape dough into loaf. Place in prepared pan. Cover and let rise in a warm place until nearly double (30 to 45 minutes).

6. Preheat oven to 375°F. Bake for 40 to 45 minutes or until bread sounds hollow when lightly tapped. (If necessary, cover loosely with foil for the last 10 minutes of baking to prevent overbrowning.) Immediately remove bread from pan. Cool on a wire rack. Makes 1 loaf (16 slices).

Maple Oatmeal Bread

You can taste two favorite breakfast items in this bread—coffee and maple syrup.

PER SLICE: 111 cal., 2 g total fat (0 g sat. fat), 13 mg chol., 151 mg sodium, 20 g carb., 2 g fiber, 4 g pro. Exchanges: 1.5 starch. Carb choices: 1.5.

5¾ to 6¼ cups all-purpose flour
2 packages active dry yeast
1½ cups prepared coffee
1 cup quick-cooking rolled oats
¾ cup maple syrup
⅓ cup butter
2 teaspoons salt
2 eggs or ½ cup refrigerated or frozen egg product, thawed
Nonstick cooking spray

1. In a very large mixing bowl combine 2 cups of the flour and the yeast. In a medium saucepan heat the coffee, rolled oats, maple syrup, butter, and salt just until warm (120° to 130°F) and butter is almost melted. Add to flour mixture along with eggs. Beat with an electric mixer on low to medium speed for 30 seconds, scraping sides of bowl constantly. Beat on high speed for 3 minutes. Using a wooden spoon, stir in as much of the remaining flour as you can.

2. Turn dough out onto a lightly floured surface. Knead in enough remaining flour to make a moderately soft dough that is smooth and elastic (3 to 5 minutes total). Shape dough into a ball. Place in a lightly greased bowl, turning once to grease surface of dough. Cover; let rise in a warm place until double in size (about 1 hour).

3. Punch dough down. Turn dough out onto a lightly floured surface. Divide dough in half. Cover; let rest for 10 minutes. Coat two 9×5×3-inch loaf pans with cooking spray; set aside.

4. Shape dough into 2 loaves by patting or rolling. To shape by patting, gently pat and pinch, tucking edges underneath. To shape by rolling, on a lightly floured surface, roll each dough half into a 12×8-inch rectangle. Roll up each rectangle, starting from a short side. Seal seams with your fingertips. Place shaped dough in prepared pans. Cover and let bread rise in a warm place until nearly double in size (30 to 45 minutes).

5. Preheat oven to 375°F. Bake about 30 minutes or until bread sounds hollow when lightly tapped (if necessary, cover loosely with foil the last 10 to 15 minutes of baking to prevent overbrowning). Immediately remove bread from pan. Cool on rack. Makes 2 loaves (28 slices).

Parmesan Corn Bread

This crunchy, flavorful corn bread makes the perfect go-with for a holiday soup supper.

PER SLICE: 150 cal., 5 g total fat (1 g sat. fat), 3 mg chol., 241 mg sodium, 22 g carb., 2 g fiber, 5 g pro. Exchanges: 1.5 starch, 0.5 fat. Carb choices: 1.5.

- ¼ cup bulgur
- 1 cup coarsely ground or regular yellow cornmeal
- 1 cup all-purpose flour
- ½ cup grated Parmesan cheese
- 2 tablespoons sugar
- 1 tablespoon baking powder
- ½ teaspoon salt
- ½ cup refrigerated or frozen egg product, thawed, or 2 eggs
- 1 cup fat-free milk
- ⅓ cup sliced green onions
- 3 tablespoons olive oil or cooking oil
- 2 tablespoons snipped fresh basil or 2 teaspoons dried basil, crushed
- Olive oil or cooking oil (optional)
- Coarsely ground or regular yellow cornmeal (optional)

1. Preheat oven to 375°F. In a small bowl, pour 1 cup *boiling water* over bulgur; let stand for 5 minutes. Generously grease and flour a 1½-quart soufflé dish or 9×5×3-inch loaf pan. Set aside.

2. In a large bowl, stir together cornmeal, flour, Parmesan cheese, sugar, baking powder, and salt. Make a well in the center.

3. In a medium bowl, beat egg slightly; stir in milk, green onions, 2 tablespoons of the oil, and basil. Drain bulgur; stir into egg mixture. Add bulgur mixture all at once to flour mixture; stir just until moistened (the batter should be lumpy).

4. Pour batter into prepared dish or pan. Bake until a wooden toothpick inserted near center comes out clean, allowing 45 to 50 minutes for the soufflé dish or 40 to 45 minutes for the loaf pan. If necessary, cover loosely with foil for the last 10 to 15 minutes of baking to prevent overbrowning.

5. Cool on a wire rack for 10 minutes. Remove from dish. Serve warm. If desired, brush with oil; sprinkle with cornmeal. Makes 1 loaf (12 slices).

Harvest Breadsticks

Top these hearty potato breadsticks with one or a combination of the various seeds and spices listed.

PER BREADSTICK: 87 cal., 1 g total fat (0 g sat. fat), 2 mg chol., 131 mg sodium, 17 g carb., 1 g fiber, 3 g pro. Exchanges: 1 starch. Carb choices: 1.

- 2 small potatoes, peeled and cubed (1⅓ cups)
- 1 cup buttermilk
- 2 tablespoons sugar
- 2 tablespoons butter or margarine
- 6 to 6½ cups all-purpose flour
- 2 packages active dry yeast
- 1 egg white
    Desired toppings such as sesame seeds, fennel seeds, dill seeds, cumin seeds, red curry powder, chili powder, and/or crushed red peppercorns (optional)

1. In a small saucepan, bring 1¼ cups *water* and potatoes to boiling. Simmer, covered, about 15 minutes or until potatoes are very tender; do not drain. Mash potatoes in water. Measure potato mixture. If necessary, add additional water to make 1⅔ cups mixture total. Return potato mixture to pan. Add buttermilk, sugar, butter, and 2 teaspoons *salt*. Heat or cool as necessary until warm (120°F to 130°F), stirring constantly.

2. In a large mixing bowl, combine 2 cups of the flour and the yeast. Add the potato mixture. Beat with an electric mixer on low to medium speed for 30 seconds, scraping the side of the bowl constantly. Beat on high speed 3 minutes. Using a wooden spoon, stir in as much of the remaining flour as you can.

3. Turn dough out onto a lightly floured surface. Knead in enough of the remaining flour to make a moderately stiff dough (6 to 8 minutes). Shape dough into a ball. Place in a lightly greased bowl, turning once to grease dough. Cover; let rise in warm place until double in size (30 to 45 minutes).

4. Punch dough down. Turn dough out onto a lightly floured surface; divide dough in half. Cover and let rest 10 minutes. Roll 1 portion to a 15×8-inch rectangle. Cut into twenty 8×¾-inch pieces. Stretch and roll each piece to form a 15-inch-long stick. Place ¾ to 1 inch apart on lightly greased baking sheets. Repeat with remaining dough.

5. Cover; let breadsticks rise 20 minutes. Preheat oven to 375°F. Stir together egg white and 1 tablespoon *water;* brush onto breadsticks. If desired, sprinkle with toppings. Bake for 15 minutes or until light brown. Transfer to a wire rack. Serve warm or at room temperature. Makes 40 breadsticks.

Harvest Breadsticks

Swiss Cheese Almond Flatbread

This cheesy flatbread is robust enough to stand alone as an appetizer, but you also can team it with a bowl of soup for a light meal.

PER SLICE: 97 cal., 3 g total fat (1 g sat. fat), 3 mg chol., 138 mg sodium, 14 g carb., 1 g fiber, 3 g pro. Exchanges: 1 starch, 0.5 fat. Carb choices: 1.

3½ to 4 cups all-purpose flour
1 package active dry yeast
1 teaspoon salt
1¼ cups warm water (120°F to 130°F)
2 tablespoons olive oil
⅔ cup finely shredded Swiss cheese
⅓ cup sliced almonds
½ teaspoon cracked black pepper
½ teaspoon coarse sea salt

1. In a large mixer bowl, stir together 1¼ cups of the flour, the yeast, and the 1 teaspoon salt. Add the warm water and 1 tablespoon of the olive oil. Beat with an electric mixer on low to medium speed for 30 seconds, scraping side of bowl. Beat on high speed for 3 minutes. Using a wooden spoon, stir in as much of the remaining flour as you can.

2. Turn out dough onto a lightly floured surface. Knead in enough of the remaining flour to make a stiff dough that is smooth and elastic (8 to 10 minutes total). Shape dough into a ball. Place in a lightly greased bowl; turn once to grease surface of dough. Cover; let rise in a warm place until double in size (about 1 hour).

3. Punch dough down. Turn out onto a lightly floured surface. Divide in half. Lightly oil 2 baking sheets. Shape each half of the dough into a ball. Place on prepared baking sheets. Cover and let rest for 10 minutes. Flatten each ball into a circle about 9 inches in diameter. Using your fingers, press ½-inch-deep indentations about 2 inches apart into the surface. Brush with the remaining 1 tablespoon olive oil. Sprinkle with cheese, almonds, pepper, and coarse salt. Cover; let rise in a warm place until nearly double in size (about 20 minutes).

4. Preheat oven to 375°F. Bake flatbread for 25 to 30 minutes or until golden brown. Remove from baking sheets; cool on wire racks. Makes 2 rounds (24 slices).

Flaxseed and Rye Breadsticks

Flaxseeds contain both soluble and insoluble fiber. Soluble fiber helps regulate blood glucose levels.

PER BREADSTICK: 134 cal., 4 g total fat (0 g sat. fat), 0 mg chol., 185 mg sodium, 21 g carb., 3 g fiber, 4 g pro. Exchanges: 1.5 starch, 0.5 fat. Carb choices: 1.5.

⅓ cup flaxseeds
2¼ to 2¾ cups all-purpose flour
1 cup rye flour
1 package active dry yeast
1½ cups warm water (120°F to 130°F)
2 tablespoons olive oil
1 tablespoon honey
1¼ teaspoons salt
   Nonstick cooking spray
2 tablespoons flaxseeds

1. Heat a large skillet over medium-low heat. Add the ⅓ cup flaxseeds; cook and stir for 5 to 7 minutes or until seeds pop; cool. In a blender, cover and blend until ground (you should have about ½ cup).

2. In a large mixer bowl, stir together 1 cup of the all-purpose flour, the rye flour, and yeast. Add warm water, oil, honey, and salt. Beat with an electric mixer on low speed for 30 seconds, scraping bowl constantly. Beat on high speed for 3 minutes. Using a wooden spoon, stir in the ground flaxseeds and as much of the remaining all-purpose flour as you can.

3. Turn out dough onto a lightly floured surface. Knead in enough of the remaining all-purpose flour to make a moderately stiff dough that is smooth and elastic (6 to 8 minutes total). Shape into a ball. Place in a lightly greased bowl; turn to grease the surface. Cover; let rise until nearly double in size (about 1 hour).

4. Punch dough down. Turn out onto a lightly floured surface. Cover; let rest for 10 minutes. Coat 2 baking sheets with cooking spray; set aside.

5. Roll dough into a 16×8-inch rectangle. Brush generously with water. Sprinkle with 2 tablespoons flaxseeds. Gently pat flaxseeds into dough. Cut dough crosswise into 1-inch-wide strips.

6. Place strips 1 inch apart on prepared baking sheets, twisting breadsticks 2 to 3 times, if desired. Cover; let rise in a warm place until nearly double in size (about 30 minutes).

7. Preheat oven to 425°F. Bake breadsticks for 12 to 15 minutes or until golden. Remove from baking sheets. Cool on wire racks. Makes 16 breadsticks.

Flaxseed and Rye Breadsticks

Orange-Rye Spirals

(why rye?)

If you've never used rye in baking, here's your chance. Rye is a cereal grain with a distinctive, robust flavor. Rye flour often is used in baking bread, but you can also serve cracked rye as a cooked breakfast cereal and in pilafs. Cooked rye berries are suitable for using in casseroles, soups, and stuffings. Store all forms of rye in an airtight container in a cool, dry place for up to 1 month. Rye flour and cracked rye keep for up to 3 months in the refrigerator or freezer. Keep rye berries for up to 5 months in the refrigerator or freezer.

Orange-Rye Spirals

Orange and caraway make these yeast rolls a memorable addition to a special holiday brunch.

PER ROLL: 164 cal., 4 g total fat (1 g sat. fat), 0 mg chol., 390 mg sodium, 29 g carb., 2 g fiber, 4 g pro. Exchanges: 1 starch, 1 carb., 0.5 fat. Carb choices: 2.

- 2¾ to 3¼ cups all-purpose flour
- 1 package active dry yeast
- 1 cup water
- ¼ cup sugar
- ¼ cup cooking oil
- ¾ teaspoon salt
- 2 egg whites
- 1¼ cups rye flour
- ¼ cup finely chopped candied orange peel
- 1 teaspoon caraway seeds, crushed
  Nonstick cooking spray
- ¼ cup low-sugar orange marmalade or orange marmalade, melted

1. In a large mixer bowl, stir together 2 cups all-purpose flour and yeast. In a medium saucepan, heat and stir water, sugar, oil, and salt just until warm (120°F to 130°F). Add water mixture and egg whites to flour mixture. Beat with an electric mixer on low to medium speed for 30 seconds, scraping side of bowl occasionally. Beat on high speed for 3 minutes. Using a wooden spoon, stir in rye flour, orange peel, caraway seeds, and as much of the remaining all-purpose flour as you can.

2. Turn out dough onto a lightly floured surface. Knead in enough of the remaining all-purpose flour to make a moderately stiff dough that is smooth and elastic (6 to 8 minutes total). Shape dough into a ball. Place in a lightly greased bowl; turn once. Cover; let rise in a warm place until double in size (about 1 to 1½ hours).

3. Punch dough down. Turn out dough onto a lightly floured surface. Divide dough in half. Cover; let rest for 10 minutes. Coat 2 baking sheets with cooking spray.

4. Divide each half of the dough into 8 pieces. On a lightly floured surface, roll each piece into a 12-inch-long rope. Form each rope into an "S" shape, coiling each end snugly. Place rolls on prepared baking sheets. Cover and let rise in a warm place until nearly double in size (about 30 minutes).

5. Preheat oven to 375°F. Bake about 14 minutes or until golden brown. Transfer to a wire rack. Cool slightly. Brush rolls with orange marmalade while warm. Serve warm. Makes 16 rolls.

Potato Parker House Rolls

Serve these rolls with butter, honey butter, or preserves.

PER ROLL: 77 cal., 3 g total fat (2 g sat. fat), 13 mg chol., 94 mg sodium, 11 g carb., 0 g fiber, 2 g pro. Exchanges: 1 starch. Carb choices: 1.

- 1 potato (about 5 ounces), peeled and cut into chunks
- 3½ to 4 cups all-purpose flour
- 1 package active dry yeast
- ¾ cup fat-free milk
- 6 tablespoons butter or margarine
- 3 tablespoons sugar
- 1 egg or ¼ cup refrigerated egg product, thawed
  Melted butter
  Nonstick cooking spray

1. In a covered saucepan, cook potato in a small amount of boiling salted water for 10 to 12 minutes or until tender; drain. Mash potato with a potato masher or beat with an electric mixer on medium speed until smooth. Measure ½ cup mashed potato; cool to room temperature. Discard remaining mashed potato.

2. In a large bowl, combine 2 cups of the flour and yeast. In a saucepan, heat and stir the ¾ cup milk, the 6 tablespoons butter, ½ cup *water*, sugar, and 1 teaspoon *salt* just until warm (120°F to 130°F). Add milk mixture to flour mixture along with egg and mashed potato. Beat with an electric mixer on low speed for 30 seconds, scraping side of bowl. Beat on high for 3 minutes. Using a wooden spoon, stir in as much remaining flour as you can.

3. Transfer dough to a lightly floured surface. Knead in enough remaining flour to make a moderately stiff dough that is smooth and elastic (6 to 8 minutes total). Shape dough into a ball. Place in a lightly greased bowl, turning once to grease surface. Cover; let dough rise in a warm place until double in size (1 to 1½ hours).

4. Punch dough down; divide in half. Cover; let rest for 10 minutes. Coat baking sheets with cooking spray; set aside. On a lightly floured surface, roll each dough half to ⅜-inch thickness. Using a floured 2½- to 2¾-inch round cutter, cut out circles. Gather scraps; set aside. Lightly brush circles with butter. With the handle of a wooden spoon, firmly press an off-center crease in each circle. Fold each circle along crease. Press folded edge firmly. Place rolls 2 to 3 inches apart on prepared sheets.

5. Gather scraps; lightly knead. Roll, cut, and shape as above. Brush rolls with *milk*. Cover with plastic wrap; let rise until almost double in size (30 minutes). Preheat oven to 375°F. Bake for 12 to 15 minutes or until golden. Transfer to a rack; cool. Serve warm. Makes 36 rolls.

holiday cookies

Raspberry-Fig Linzer Cookies

Gather your children, grandchildren, or kids at heart in the kitchen for a snowy afternoon of *baking* and *decorating* cookies that everyone can enjoy. Our Test Kitchen has come up with ways to make *cookies* that taste great and that you can eat, too—just like the ones you remember baking with your own *grandmother*.

Raspberry-Fig Linzer Cookies

These pretty cookies showcase a crimson raspberry and fig filling in the "window" of the top cookie.

PER 2-INCH COOKIE: 65 cal., 2 g total fat (1 g sat. fat), 2 mg chol., 27 mg sodium, 11 g carb., 0 g fiber, 1 g pro. Exchanges: 1 carb., 0.5 fat. Carb choices: 1.

PER COOKIE WITH SUBSTITUTE: same as above, except 62 cal., 10 g carb. Exchanges: 0.5 carb. Carb choices: 0.5.

- 2 tablespoons butter, softened
- ¼ cup granulated sugar or sugar-substitute blend* equivalent to ¼ cup sugar
- ½ teaspoon baking powder
- 2 tablespoons cooking oil
- ¼ cup refrigerated egg product or 1 egg
- ½ teaspoon vanilla
- 2 cups sifted cake flour
- 3 tablespoons yellow or white cornmeal
- 1 recipe Raspberry-Fig Filling (see recipe, page 122)
  Powdered sugar

1. In a mixing bowl, beat butter, sugar, baking powder, and ⅛ teaspoon *salt* with a mixer on medium speed until combined. Beat in oil, egg, and vanilla until combined. Beat in as much flour as you can. Stir in remaining flour and cornmeal. Halve dough. Wrap; chill for 2 hours.

2. Preheat oven to 375°F. On a lightly floured surface, roll each dough portion to ⅛-inch thickness. Using a 1½- to 2-inch cookie cutter, cut into desired shapes. Using a ¾- to 1-inch cutter, cut out centers of half of the cutouts. Arrange shapes 1 inch apart on ungreased cookie sheets. Bake about 5 minutes or just until edges are firm. Transfer to a wire rack; cool.

3. Spread Raspberry-Fig Filling onto each whole cookie. Sprinkle remaining cookies with powdered sugar; place on top of filled cookies. Makes about 26 (2-inch) or 46 (1½-inch) sandwich cookies.

*Sugar Substitutes: Choose from Splenda Sugar Blend for Baking or Equal Sugar Lite. Follow package directions for product amount equal to ¼ cup sugar.

Raspberry-Fig Filling

Use this filling for the Linzer cookies.
Fresh or frozen raspberries work equally well.

⅓ cup orange juice

⅓ cup fresh or frozen red raspberries

3 tablespoons finely snipped dried figs

1 recipe Raspberry-Fig Linzer Cookies (see page 121)

1. In a small saucepan, combine orange juice, raspberries, and figs. Bring to boiling; reduce heat.

2. Simmer, uncovered, for 5 to 7 minutes or until mixture is thickened, stirring frequently. Remove from heat. Transfer mixture to a blender or food processor. Cover and blend or process until nearly smooth. Cool completely. Use in Raspberry-Fig Linzer Cookies. Makes about ½ cup.

Sugar Cookie Cutouts

Decorating cookies with Cream Cheese Frosting with reduced-fat cream cheese and butter flavoring in place of butter helps keep fat in check.

PER COOKIE (NOT DECORATED): 48 cal., 2 g total fat (1 g sat. fat), 3 mg chol., 26 mg sodium, 6 g carb., 0 g fiber, 1 g pro. Exchanges: 0.5 carb., 0.5 fat. Carb choices: 0.5.

PER COOKIE WITH SUBSTITUTE: same as above, except 44 cal., 5 g carb. Carb choices: 0.

¼ cup butter, softened

½ cup sugar or sugar-substitute blend* equivalent to ½ cup sugar

1 teaspoon baking powder

¼ teaspoon salt

¼ cup cooking oil

¼ cup refrigerated or frozen egg product, thawed, or 1 egg

1 teaspoon vanilla

2½ cups sifted cake flour

1 recipe Cream Cheese Frosting (see right) (optional)

1. In a large mixing bowl, beat butter with an electric mixer on medium speed for 30 seconds. Beat in sugar, baking powder, and salt. Add oil, egg, and vanilla; beat until combined. Beat in as much of the flour as you can. Stir in any remaining flour. Divide dough in half. Cover; chill for 1 to 2 hours or until easy to handle.

2. Preheat oven to 375°F. On a lightly floured surface, roll dough, half at a time, to ⅛-inch thickness. Using a 2½-inch cookie cutter, cut into desired shapes. Place cutouts 1 inch apart on ungreased cookie sheets. Reroll scraps as needed.

3. Bake for 6 to 8 minutes or until edges are firm and just starting to brown. Transfer to a wire rack; cool. If desired, frost with Cream Cheese Frosting and decorate. Makes about 48 cookies.

*Sugar Substitutes: Choose from Splenda Sugar Blend for Baking or Equal Sugar Lite. Follow package directions to use product amount equivalent to ½ cup sugar.

Cream Cheese Frosting

If you like, thin this frosting with fat-free milk to make it a drizzling consistency and add food coloring for tints. Use it for Sugar Cookie Cutouts, left.

PER TEASPOON: 28 cal., 0 g total fat (0 g sat. fat), 1 mg chol., 8 mg sodium, 6 g carb., 0 g fiber, 0 g pro. Exchanges: 0.5 carb. Carb choices: 0.5.

½ of an 8-ounce package reduced-fat cream cheese (Neufchâtel), softened

1 teaspoon vanilla

½ teaspoon butter flavoring (optional)

3 to 3½ cups powdered sugar*

Food coloring (optional)

1. In a large mixing bowl, beat cream cheese, vanilla, and butter flavoring (if using) with electric mixer on medium speed until very smooth. Gradually beat in enough powdered sugar to make a frosting of spreading or piping consistency. If desired, tint frosting with food coloring. Makes about 1¼ cups (sixty 1-teaspoon servings).

Chocolate Cream Cheese Frosting: Beat in 2 tablespoons unsweetened cocoa powder with vanilla. Reduce powdered sugar to 2½ to 3 cups.

Mint Cream Cheese Frosting: Add ¼ teaspoon mint extract with vanilla.

Coffee Cream Cheese Frosting: Add 2 teaspoons instant coffee crystals with the vanilla.

*Sugar Substitutes: We don't recommend using a sugar substitute for this recipe.

Sugar Cookie Cutouts

Soft Snickerdoodles

Soft Snickerdoodles

This cookie classic is updated with whole wheat flour, dried fruit, and peanuts. Kids might like it even more!

PER COOKIE: 96 cal., 5 g total fat (2 g sat. fat), 9 mg chol., 68 mg sodium, 13 g carb., 1 g fiber, 2 g pro. Exchanges: 1 carb., 1 fat. Carb choices: 1.
PER COOKIE WITH SUBSTITUTE: same as above, except 89 cal., 10 g carb. Exchanges: 0.5 carb., 1 fat. Carb choices: 0.5.

1½ cups sugar or sugar substitute baking blend* equivalent to 1½ cups sugar
3 teaspoons ground cinnamon
1 cup butter, softened
¾ cup refrigerated or frozen egg product, thawed, or 3 eggs
2 teaspoons vanilla
2 cups all-purpose flour
¾ cup whole wheat flour
2 teaspoons cream of tartar
1 teaspoon baking soda
¼ teaspoon salt
1 cup chopped peanuts
1 cup dried currants
1 6-ounce package dried cranberries (1 cup)

1. Preheat oven to 400°F. In a small bowl, combine 2 tablespoons of the sugar or substitute and 1 teaspoon of the cinnamon; set aside.

2. In a large mixing bowl, combine butter and the remaining sugar or substitute; beat with an electric mixer on medium speed until combined. Add egg and vanilla; beat until combined.

3. In a medium bowl, stir together flours, cream of tartar, baking soda, the remaining 2 teaspoons cinnamon, and salt. Add to beaten mixture; beat until mixed. Stir in peanuts, currants, and cranberries.

4. Drop dough by rounded teaspoons 2 inches apart onto ungreased cookie sheets. Sprinkle with cinnamon-sugar mixture.

5. Bake for 7 to 8 minutes or until light brown. Transfer to wire racks; cool. Makes about 60 cookies.

*Sugar Substitutes: Choose from Splenda Sugar Blend for Baking or Equal Sugar Lite. Follow the package directions to use the product amount equivalent to 1½ cups sugar.

Almond Fudge Rounds (back)
and Mint Fudge Rounds (front)

Almond Fudge Rounds

You'll love both versions of this fancy cookie.

PER ALMOND FUDGE ROUND: 73 cal., 3 g total fat (1 g sat. fat), 5 mg chol., 46 mg sodium, 10 g carb., 0 g fiber, 2 g pro. Exchanges: 0.5 carb., 0.5 fat. Carb choices: 0.5.

PER ALMOND FUDGE ROUND WITH SUBSTITUTE: same as above, except 66 cal., 44 mg sodium, 8 g carb.

- ⅓ cup butter, softened
- ¾ cup packed brown sugar or brown sugar-substitute blend* equivalent to ¾ cup brown sugar
- 1 teaspoon instant espresso coffee powder
- ¾ teaspoon baking soda
- 2 egg whites
- ⅓ cup plain low-fat yogurt
- ½ teaspoon almond extract
- ⅔ cup unsweetened cocoa powder
- 1½ cups all-purpose flour or white whole wheat flour
- 1 ounce white baking chocolate squares (with cocoa butter)
- ¼ teaspoon shortening
- 36 to 40 whole almonds, toasted

1. In a large mixing bowl, beat butter with an electric mixer on medium to high speed for 30 seconds. Add brown sugar, espresso powder, and baking soda; beat until combined, scraping bowl occasionally. Add egg whites, yogurt, and almond extract; beat until combined. Beat in cocoa powder. Beat in as much of the flour as you can with the mixer. Using a wooden spoon, stir in any remaining flour. If necessary, cover and chill dough for 1 to 2 hours or until easy to handle.

2. Preheat oven to 350°F. Shape dough into 1-inch balls. Place 2 inches apart on ungreased cookie sheets. Bake for 6 to 8 minutes or just until edges are firm.

3. Using the back of a small round measuring spoon, immediately make an indentation in the center of each warm cookie. Transfer cookies to a wire rack; cool.

4. In a small saucepan, heat and stir white baking chocolate and shortening over low heat until melted and smooth. Dip each almond halfway into chocolate mixture. Place an almond into the indentation in each cookie. Let stand until chocolate is set. Makes about 36 cookies.

*Sugar Substitutes: Use Splenda Brown Sugar Blend to substitute for brown sugar. Follow package directions to use the amount equivalent to ¾ cup brown sugar.

Mint Fudge Rounds: Prepare as directed, except substitute mint extract for almond extract; omit almonds and indentations. After placing dough balls on cookie sheets, use the bottom of a glass lightly coated with nonstick spray to slightly flatten. Bake as directed. Drizzle with melted chocolate. If desired, garnish each cookie with a fresh mint leaf.

Apricot-Ginger Pinwheels

Prepare these swirls one day, then bake them the next.

PER COOKIE: 63 cal., 3 g total fat (1 g sat. fat), 5 mg chol., 36 mg sodium, 9 g carb., 1 g fiber, 1 g pro. Exchanges: 0.5 carb., 0.5 fat. Carb choices: 0.5.

PER COOKIE WITH SUBSTITUTE: same as above, except 57 cal., 35 mg sodium, 8 g carb.

- ¾ cup dried apricot halves, finely snipped
- 1 tablespoon granulated sugar or sugar substitute* equivalent to 1 tablespoon sugar
- ¾ teaspoon ground ginger
- ⅓ cup butter, softened
- ⅓ cup packed brown sugar or brown sugar-substitute blend* equivalent to ⅓ cup brown sugar
- ¼ teaspoon baking soda
- ⅛ teaspoon salt
- 1 egg white
- 2 tablespoons fat-free milk
- ½ teaspoon vanilla
- 1 cup whole wheat flour
- ½ cup all-purpose flour
- ⅓ cup finely chopped pistachio nuts
  Nonstick cooking spray

1. For filling, in a small saucepan, combine apricots, ¼ cup *water,* granulated sugar, and ¼ teaspoon of the ginger. Bring to boiling; reduce heat. Cook and stir for 1 minute. Cover; cool completely.

2. In a large mixing bowl, beat butter with an electric mixer on medium to high speed for 30 seconds. Add brown sugar, the remaining ½ teaspoon ginger, the baking soda, and salt; beat until combined, scraping bowl occasionally. Beat in egg white, milk, and vanilla until combined. Beat in as much of the whole wheat flour and all-purpose flour as you can with the mixer. Using a wooden spoon, stir in remaining flours.

3. Roll dough between 2 pieces of waxed paper or parchment paper into a 12×10-inch rectangle. Remove top sheet of paper. Spread apricot filling onto dough, leaving a ½-inch border around edges. Starting at a long side, roll up dough. Pinch edges of dough to seal.

4. Spread nuts on a large piece of waxed paper or parchment paper. Roll dough pinwheel in the nuts to evenly coat the outside, pressing nuts in gently so they stick to the dough. Wrap dough in waxed paper or plastic wrap. Chill for 2 hours.

5. Preheat oven to 375°F. Coat a cookie sheet with nonstick cooking spray. Cut dough pinwheel into ¼-inch-thick slices. Place slices 1 inch apart on prepared cookie sheet. Bake for 8 to 10 minutes or until edges are light brown. Transfer cookies to a wire rack; cool. Makes about 32 cookies.

*Sugar Substitutes: For the granulated sugar substitute, choose from Splenda granular, Equal Spoonful or packets, or Sweet'N Low bulk or packets. For the brown sugar substitute, use Splenda Brown Sugar Blend. Follow package directions to use product amounts equivalent to 1 tablespoon granulated sugar and ⅓ cup brown sugar.

Make-Ahead Directions: Prepare pinwheel logs as directed through Step 4. Wrap tightly and chill for up to 24 hours before slicing and baking as directed.

Oatmeal Cookies

Reduced-fat peanut butter gives this classic any-day cookie lots of flavor but just a little fat.

PER COOKIE: 76 cal., 4 g total fat (2 g sat. fat), 7 mg chol., 69 mg sodium, 9 g carb., 1 g fiber, 2 g pro. Exchanges: 0.5 carb., 0.5 fat. Carb choices: 0.5.

- ½ cup butter, softened
- ½ cup reduced-fat peanut butter
- ⅓ cup granulated sugar*
- ⅓ cup packed brown sugar*
- ½ teaspoon baking soda
- 2 egg whites
- ½ teaspoon vanilla
- 1 cup all-purpose flour
- 1 cup quick-cooking rolled oats

1. Preheat oven to 375°F. In a large mixing bowl, combine butter and peanut butter. Beat with an electric mixer on medium to high speed about 30 seconds or until combined.

2. Add granulated sugar, brown sugar, and baking soda. Beat until combined, scraping bowl occasionally. Beat in egg whites and vanilla until combined. Beat in as much of the flour as you can with the mixer. Using a wooden spoon, stir in any remaining flour. Stir in oats.

3. Drop dough by rounded teaspoons 2 inches apart on ungreased cookie sheets. Bake for 7 to 8 minutes or until edges are golden brown. Cool on cookie sheet for 1 minute. Transfer cookies to a wire rack; cool. Makes about 40 cookies.

*Sugar Substitutes: We don't recommend using a sugar substitute for this recipe.

(cookie strategies)

Use these tips to make home-baked cookies more healthful.

1. **Reduce saturated fat** by using canola oil in place of some of the butter.
2. **Choose a sugar substitute** that's appropriate for baking. Because sugar tenderizes, browns, and crisps cookies, a sugar-substitute blend works better than a plain substitute.
3. **Switch to cake flour** to make cookies more tender.
4. **Substitute reduced-fat cream cheese** for some of the butter in cookies and frostings.
5. **Incorporate whole grains** to increase cookies' fiber content. Fiber helps stabilize blood glucose.
6. **Use cocoa powder** instead of melted chocolate. This reduces the fat content and lets you use less flour, which lowers the carb count.
7. **Make your own fillings** so you can lower the level of sugar or use a sugar substitute.
8. **Opt for dried fruits** instead of candied fruits.
9. **Include a moderate amount** of healthful nuts, especially walnuts, almonds, and pecans.
10. **Try citrus peel,** extracts, and spices for flavor.

Apricot-Ginger Pinwheels

Cranberry-Hazelnut Tarts

(pearl of a fruit)

The holidays just wouldn't be the holidays without cranberries, and with good reason. Research has shown that compounds in cranberries play a roll in controlling diabetes, promoting dental health, and preventing heart disease and cancer. In particular, cranberries contain anthocyanins, antioxidants that prevent the damage from free radicals that occurs in diabetes. So go ahead and savor this nugget of nutrition in your holiday baking and include cranberry juice in your daily meal plan.

Cranberry-Hazelnut Tarts

A cinnamon-spiced shell cradles cranberries and nuts for a bite-size gem on a cookie tray.

PER TART: 83 cal., 4 g total fat (2 g sat. fat), 9 mg chol., 60 mg sodium, 11 g carb., 1 g fiber, 1 g pro. Exchanges: 0.5 carb., 1 fat. Carb choices: 1.

- ⅔ cup quick-cooking rolled oats
- ½ cup whole wheat flour
- ¼ cup all-purpose flour
- ½ of an 8-ounce package reduced-fat cream cheese (Neufchâtel), softened
- ¼ cup butter, softened
- ¼ cup packed brown sugar*
- ¼ teaspoon baking soda
- ¼ teaspoon ground cinnamon
- ⅛ teaspoon salt
- ¼ cup hazelnuts, toasted** and chopped
- 1 recipe Cranberry-Hazelnut Filling (see below)

1. Preheat oven to 350°F. For dough, in a small bowl, combine oats, whole wheat flour, and all-purpose flour.

2. In a large mixing bowl, beat cream cheese and butter with an electric mixer on medium to high speed for 30 seconds. Add the ¼ cup brown sugar, baking soda, ¼ teaspoon cinnamon, and salt; beat until combined. Beat in as much of the oat mixture as you can with the mixer. Using a wooden spoon, stir in remaining oat mixture.

3. Divide dough evenly among twenty-four 1¾-inch muffin cups. Press onto bottom and up sides of cups.

4. Spoon Cranberry-Hazelnut Filling evenly into dough-lined cups. Sprinkle with 2 tablespoons of the hazelnuts. Bake for 15 to 20 minutes or until edges of crusts are golden. Cool in cups for 5 minutes. Remove tarts from cups; cool on a wire rack. Makes 24 tarts.

Cranberry-Hazelnut Filling: In a small saucepan, combine ⅓ cup brown sugar, 2 teaspoons cornstarch, and ½ teaspoon ground cinnamon. Add 1¼ cups fresh cranberries and ⅔ cup water. Cook and stir over medium heat until thickened and bubbly. Stir in 2 tablespoons of the hazelnuts.

***Sugar Substitutes:** We don't recommend using brown sugar substitute for this recipe.

****Test Kitchen Tip:** To toast hazelnuts, preheat oven to 350°F. Place nuts in a shallow baking pan. Bake about 10 minutes or until toasted, stirring once or twice so nuts don't burn. Place warm nuts on a clean kitchen towel. Rub nuts with towel to remove the loose skins.

Lemon Gingersnaps

You can also top the mousse with mandarin orange sections or fresh raspberries instead of the kumquats.

PER COOKIE: 42 cal., 1 g total fat (0 g sat. fat), 0 mg chol., 72 mg sodium, 8 g carb., 1 g fiber, 1 g pro. Exchanges: 0.5 carb. Carb choices: 0.5.

- ½ of a 4-serving-size package sugar-free lemon-flavored gelatin (1¼ teaspoons)
- ⅓ cup boiling water
- ¼ cup cold water
- ½ of an 8-ounce package fat-free cream cheese, softened
- ½ cup frozen fat-free whipped dessert topping, thawed
- 30 purchased small gingersnaps
  Sliced fresh kumquats and/or orange peel strips

1. Line a 7½×3½×2-inch loaf pan with plastic wrap; set aside. Place gelatin in a small bowl; add the boiling water and stir to dissolve. Stir in the cold water.

2. In a medium mixing bowl, beat cream cheese with an electric mixer on medium speed until fluffy; gradually beat in gelatin mixture on low speed until combined. Fold in whipped dessert topping. Pour into prepared pan. Cover and chill for 4 to 24 hours or until set.

3. Using the plastic wrap, lift mousse out of pan. Cut in half lengthwise; then cut crosswise into ¼-inch-thick slices. If desired, cut into shapes using small cookie cutters or hors d'oeuvres cutters.

4. To serve, place one slice of the mousse on top of each gingersnap. Top with kumquat slices and/or orange peel strips. (Assemble only as many as you need at one time.) Makes 30 cookies.

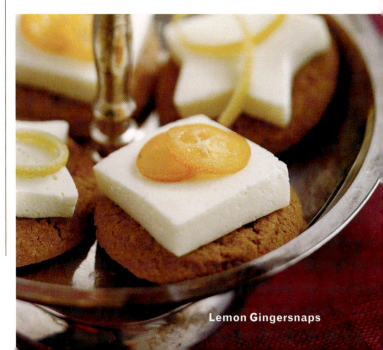

Lemon Gingersnaps

All-Star Peanut Butter Cookies.

Three ingredients? The kids can make these!

PER COOKIE: 66 cal., 4 g total fat (1 g sat. fat), 6 mg chol., 35 mg sodium, 7 g carb., 0 g fiber, 2 g pro. Exchanges: 0.5 carb., 0.5 fat. Carb choices: 0.5.

- 1 cup sugar*
- 1 cup peanut butter
- 1 egg or ¼ cup refrigerated or frozen egg product, thawed
- Sugar*

1. Preheat oven to 375°F. Grease cookie sheets; set aside. In a medium bowl, stir together the 1 cup sugar, the peanut butter, and egg until mixed.

2. Using your hands, roll peanut butter mixture into 1-inch balls; arrange 2 inches apart on prepared cookie sheets. Lightly grease a drinking glass; dip into sugar. Using glass, flatten each ball slightly. Lightly grease a small star-shape cookie cutter; dip into sugar. Press a star indentation into the center of each cookie.

3. Bake about 9 minutes or until edges are set and bottoms are light brown. Makes 36 cookies.

*Sugar Substitutes: We don't recommend using a sugar substitute for this recipe.

Brownie Cookies

Give yourself a present—a delightful chocolate treat.

PER COOKIE: 73 cal., 2 g total fat (1 g sat. fat), 6 mg chol., 38 mg sodium, 12 g carb., 0 g fiber, 1 g pro. Exchanges: 1 carb., Carb choices: 1.

- 1 cup all-purpose flour
- ¼ teaspoon baking soda
- ¼ cup butter
- ⅔ cup granulated sugar*
- ⅓ cup unsweetened cocoa powder
- ¼ cup packed brown sugar*
- ¼ cup buttermilk or sour milk**
- 1 teaspoon vanilla
- Nonstick cooking spray
- 1 tablespoon sifted powdered sugar

1. In a small bowl, stir together flour and baking soda; set aside. In a medium saucepan, melt butter; remove from heat. Stir in granulated sugar, cocoa powder, and brown sugar. Stir in buttermilk and vanilla. Stir in flour mixture just until combined. Cover and chill dough for 1 hour. (Dough will be stiff.)

2. Preheat oven to 350°F. Lightly coat cookie sheets with nonstick cooking spray. Drop chilled dough by rounded teaspoons onto cookie sheet.

3. Bake for 8 to 10 minutes or until edges are set. Cool on sheet for 1 minute. Transfer to a wire rack; cool. Sprinkle with powdered sugar. Makes 24 cookies.

*Sugar Substitutes: We don't recommend using a sugar substitute for this recipe.

**Test Kitchen Tip: To make ¼ cup sour milk, place ¾ teaspoon lemon juice or vinegar in a glass measuring cup. Add enough milk to make ¼ cup total liquid; stir. Let mixture stand for 5 minutes before using.

Mocha Meringue Stars

These delicate drops look like holiday decorations.

PER COOKIE: 32 cal., 1 g total fat (0 g sat. fat), 0 mg chol., 7 mg sodium, 5 g carb., 0 g fiber, 1 g pro. Exchanges: 0.5 starch. Carb choices: 0.5.

- ⅓ cup sifted powdered sugar
- 2 tablespoons unsweetened cocoa powder
- 1 tablespoon cornstarch
- 1 teaspoon instant espresso coffee powder or 2 teaspoons instant coffee powder
- 3 egg whites
- ½ teaspoon vanilla
- ¼ cup granulated sugar*
- ⅓ cup semisweet chocolate pieces
- 1 teaspoon shortening

1. Preheat oven to 250°F. Line a cookie sheet with parchment paper or foil; set aside. In a small bowl, stir together powdered sugar, cocoa powder, cornstarch, and espresso powder; set mixture aside.

2. In a mixing bowl, beat egg whites and vanilla with an electric mixer on high speed until foamy. Add granulated sugar, 1 tablespoon at a time, beating until stiff peaks form. Gradually fold in cocoa mixture.

3. Transfer the mixture to a pastry bag fitted with a large star tip. Pipe twenty-four 2-inch stars onto prepared cookie sheet. (Or drop by rounded teaspoons onto prepared cookie sheet.)

4. Bake for 1 hour. Cool on cookie sheet on wire rack. When cool, carefully remove from parchment paper.

5. In a small saucepan, combine chocolate pieces and shortening. Cook and stir over low heat until melted. Drizzle chocolate over cookies. Makes 24 cookies.

*Sugar Substitutes: We don't recommend using a sugar substitute for this recipe.

Lemon Cardamom Meringue Cookies

To store, place these airy cookies in an airtight container for 3 days at room temperature or freeze for up to 3 months.

PER COOKIE: 9 cal., 0 g total fat (0 g sat. fat), 0 mg chol., 6 mg sodium, 2 g carb., 0 g fiber, 0 g pro. Exchanges: free. Carb choices: 0.

- **3 egg whites**
- **¼ cup sugar***
- **1 tablespoon cornstarch**
- **⅛ teaspoon ground cardamom**
- **½ teaspoon vanilla**
- **¼ teaspoon cream of tartar**
- **1 teaspoon finely shredded lemon, lime, or orange peel**

1. Let egg whites stand at room temperature for 30 minutes. Line a very large cookie sheet (or two smaller cookie sheets) with parchment paper or foil. In a bowl, stir together sugar, cornstarch, and cardamom.

2. Preheat oven to 300°F. In a medium mixing bowl, combine egg whites, vanilla, and cream of tartar. Beat with an electric mixer on high speed until soft peaks form (tips curl). Gradually add the sugar mixture, 1 tablespoon at a time, beating on high speed until stiff peaks form (tips stand straight). Fold in citrus peel.

3. Spoon mixture into a pastry bag fitted with an extra-large star tip. Pipe mixture into 30 swirls on prepared cookie sheet(s), making each about 2 inches in diameter and 1½ inches tall, leaving a 1½-inch space between swirls. (Or spoon mixture into a resealable plastic bag. Snip off one corner. Pipe into 30 mounds.)

4. Bake for 20 minutes (if using 2 cookie sheets, bake at the same time on separate oven racks). Turn off oven. Let cookies dry in oven, with door closed, for 30 minutes. Remove from oven and gently peel off the parchment paper or foil. Makes 30 cookies.

***Sugar Substitutes:** We don't recommend using a sugar substitute for this recipe.

Lemon Cardamom Meringue Cookies

Vanilla Biscotti

Celebrate with a cup of coffee and these crunchy cookies.

PER COOKIE: 63 cal., 2 g total fat (1 g sat. fat), 19 mg chol., 61 mg sodium, 9 g carb., 0 g fiber, 1 g pro. Exchanges: 0.5 carb., 0.5 fat. Carb choices: 0.5.

- 3 **cups all-purpose flour**
- 1 **tablespoon baking powder**
- ¼ **teaspoon salt**
- 3 **eggs**
- ¾ **cup sugar***
- ½ **cup butter, melted and cooled**
- 2 **teaspoons vanilla**
- **Nonstick cooking spray**

1. Preheat oven to 325°F. Coat a cookie sheet with nonstick cooking spray; set aside. In a bowl, combine flour, baking powder, and salt; set aside. In a mixing bowl, beat eggs with an electric mixer on high for 1 minute. Gradually beat in sugar, beating on high for 1 minute. Add butter and vanilla; beat on low speed until combined. Beat in as much of flour mixture as you can with mixer. Using a wooden spoon, stir in remaining flour mixture.

2. Divide dough into thirds. On a lightly floured surface, roll each third into a 14-inch-long roll. Arrange rolls 2½ inches apart on a prepared cookie sheet; flatten rolls slightly to 1½-inch widths. Bake about 25 minutes or until firm and light brown. Cool on cookie sheet for 15 minutes.

3. Preheat oven to 350°F. On a large cutting board, use a serrated knife to cut rolls diagonally into ½-inch-thick slices. Arrange, cut sides down, on cookie sheet. Bake for 10 minutes. Turn slices; bake about 10 minutes more or until crisp. Cool on cookie sheet. Makes 48.

***Sugar Substitutes:** We don't recommend using a sugar substitute for this recipe.

Coffee 'n' Cream Biscotti

Take time to relax and enjoy a flavorful reward.

PER COOKIE: 89 cal., 3 g total fat (2 g sat. fat), 5 mg chol., 51 mg sodium, 14 g carb., 0 g fiber, 2 g pro. Exchanges: 1 carb., 0.5 fat. Carb choices: 1.

- ¼ cup butter, softened
- ¼ of an 8-ounce package reduced-fat cream cheese (Neufchâtel), softened
- ⅔ cup sugar*
- 1 tablespoon baking powder
- ¾ cup refrigerated or frozen egg product, thawed, or 3 eggs
- 1 teaspoon vanilla
- 2½ cups all-purpose flour
- 2 tablespoons unsweetened cocoa powder
- 2 tablespoons instant espresso coffee powder
- 2 tablespoons all-purpose flour
- ½ cup semisweet chocolate pieces and/or white baking pieces

1. Preheat oven to 375°F. In a large mixing bowl, beat butter and cream cheese with an electric mixer on medium to high speed 30 seconds. Add sugar and baking powder; beat until combined, scraping bowl occasionally. Add egg and vanilla; beat until combined. Beat in as much of the 2½ cups flour as you can. Using a wooden spoon, stir in any remaining flour.

2. Divide dough in half; transfer one portion to a medium bowl. In a small bowl, combine cocoa powder and espresso powder; add to dough in bowl. Knead until combined. Add the 2 tablespoons flour to the remaining portion of dough; knead until combined.

3. Divide each dough portion in half. Shape each portion into a rope about 12 inches long. Twist together a chocolate rope and a plain rope. Gently roll twisted ropes together to form a 14-inch-long rope. Pat to make a log about 2 inches wide. Repeat with the remaining two ropes to make 2 logs. Place logs about 4 inches apart on an ungreased large baking sheet.

4. Bake about 18 minutes or until light brown. Cool on cookie sheet for 1 hour.

5. Preheat oven to 325°F. Transfer baked logs to a cutting board. Bias-slice logs into ½-inch-thick slices. Place slices on the same cookie sheet. Bake in the 325°F oven for 8 minutes. Turn slices; bake for 8 to 10 minutes more or until crisp and light brown. Transfer cookies to a wire rack; cool.

6. For a chocolate drizzle, in a small saucepan, heat semisweet chocolate pieces over low heat until melted. (If using both semisweet chocolate and white baking pieces, melt in separate saucepans.) Cool slightly. Drizzle semisweet and/or white chocolate onto cooled biscotti. Let cookies stand until chocolate is set. Makes about 32 cookies.

*Sugar Substitutes: We don't recommend using a sugar substitute for this recipe.

Tarragon Biscotti

Tarragon's light licorice flavor adds spark to these cookies.

PER COOKIE: 113 cal., 6 g total fat (2 g sat. fat), 8 mg chol., 66 mg sodium, 14 g carb., 1 g fiber, 2 g pro. Exchanges: 1 carb., 1 fat. Carb choices: 1.

- Nonstick cooking spray
- 3¼ cups all-purpose flour
- 2 teaspoons baking powder
- ½ cup butter, softened
- ⅔ cup sugar*
- ¼ cup snipped fresh tarragon
- 1 tablespoon finely shredded lemon peel
- ¼ teaspoon salt
- ¾ cup refrigerated or frozen egg product, thawed, or 3 eggs
- 1 cup chopped walnuts

1. Preheat oven to 375°F. Coat a cookie sheet with nonstick cooking spray; set aside. In a small bowl, stir together flour and baking powder; set aside.

2. In a large mixing bowl, beat butter with an electric mixer on medium to high speed for 30 seconds. Add sugar, tarragon, peel, and salt; beat until combined.

3. Beat in egg until combined. Beat in as much of the flour mixture as you can with the mixer. Using a spoon, stir in any remaining flour mixture and the walnuts.

4. Divide the dough in half. Shape each half into an 11-inch loaf. On prepared cookie sheet, place the loaves about 5 inches apart. Flatten each loaf slightly until each is 2 inches wide.

5. Bake for 20 to 25 minutes or until tops are light brown. Cool loaves on cookie sheet on wire rack about 1 hour or until completely cool.

6. Preheat oven to 325°F. Transfer loaves to a cutting board. Cut each crosswise diagonally into ¾-inch-thick slices. Arrange on ungreased cookie sheets. Bake in the 325°F oven for 10 minutes. Turn over slices; bake for 10 to 12 minutes more or until crisp. Remove from cookie sheets; cool on wire racks. Makes 32 cookies.

*Sugar Substitutes: We don't recommend using a sugar substitute for this recipe.

celebration desserts

Plum-Pear
Phyllo Bundles

No *holiday feast* is complete without dessert, whether it's a tart, pie, cheesecake, pudding, or cake. You'll find them all here, brimming with a *cornucopia* of holiday flavors: pumpkin, cranberry, cherry, apple, and, of course, *chocolate.* You can make most of these *treats* ahead for your dinner or *dessert buffet.*

Plum-Pear Phyllo Bundles

To cut fat and calories, nonstick cooking spray replaces butter between the layers of phyllo.

PER BUNDLE: 141 cal., 5 g total fat (1 g sat. fat), 5 mg chol., 98 mg sodium, 23 g carb., 2 g fiber, 2 g pro. Exchanges: 0.5 fruit, 1 carb., 1 fat. Carb choices: 1.5.

- 1 teaspoon butter
- ½ of a medium pear, cored and coarsely chopped
- ¼ cup coarsely chopped fresh plums or 2 tablespoons coarsely chopped pitted dried plums
- 1½ teaspoons honey
- ¼ teaspoon ground cardamom or ground ginger
- 1 tablespoon coarsely chopped pistachio nuts
- 3 sheets frozen phyllo dough (14×9-inch rectangles), thawed
- Nonstick cooking spray

1. In a small nonstick skillet, melt butter over medium heat. Add pear, plums, honey, and cardamom; cook and stir about 5 minutes or until fruit begins to soften. Remove from heat; let cool. Stir in pistachio nuts.

2. Preheat oven to 375°F. Line a baking sheet with foil; set aside. Unfold phyllo dough; remove one sheet of the phyllo dough. (As you work, cover the remaining phyllo dough with plastic wrap to prevent it from drying out.) Lightly coat the phyllo sheet with nonstick cooking spray. Place a second sheet of phyllo dough on top of the first; lightly coat with nonstick cooking spray. Top stack with a third sheet of phyllo dough and lightly coat with nonstick cooking spray. Cut phyllo stack in half crosswise to form two 9×7-inch rectangles.

3. Divide fruit mixture between phyllo rectangles, placing fruit in center of each rectangle. For each bundle, bring together the four corners of a phyllo rectangle; pinch gently and twist slightly to make a bundle. Place on prepared baking sheet. Lightly coat the tops of bundles with nonstick cooking spray.

4. Bake for 15 to 20 minutes or until golden. Transfer bundles to a wire rack; cool slightly. Serve warm or cool. Makes 2 bundles.

Tiramisu

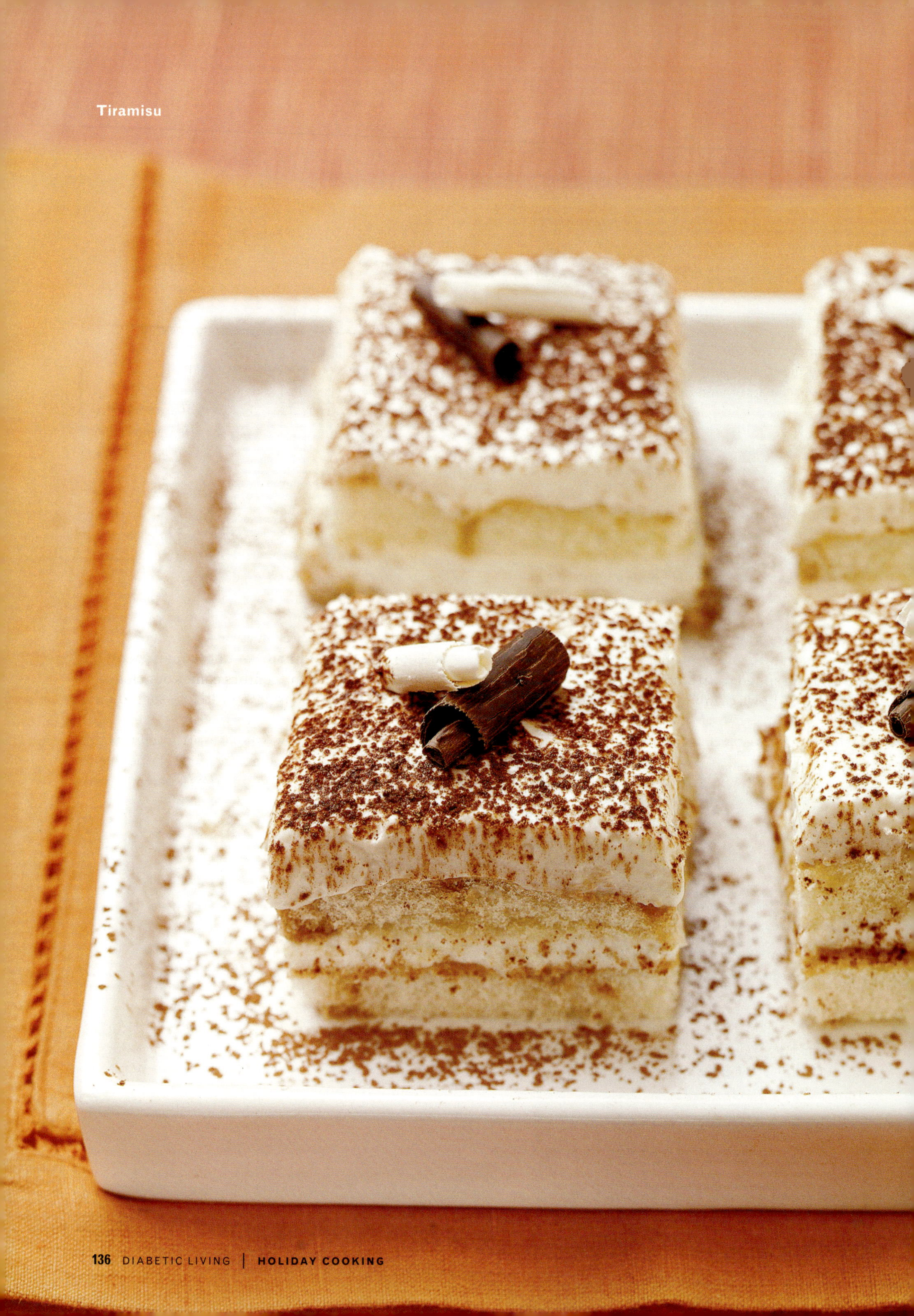

Tiramisu

Fool your guests with this lighter knockoff of the creamy classic Italian coffee-flavored dessert.

PER SERVING: 186 cal., 8 g total fat (5 g sat. fat), 67 mg chol., 182 mg sodium, 22 g carb., 0 g fiber, 5 g pro. Exchanges: 1.5 carb., 1.5 fat. Carb choices: 1.5.

- 2 8-ounce cartons fat-free dairy sour cream or light dairy sour cream
- 2 8-ounce packages reduced-fat cream cheese (Neufchâtel), softened
- ⅔ cup sugar
- ¼ cup fat-free milk
- ½ teaspoon vanilla
- ½ cup strong coffee
- 2 tablespoons coffee liqueur or strong coffee
- 2 3-ounce packages ladyfingers, split
- 2 tablespoons sifted unsweetened cocoa powder
  Unsweetened cocoa powder (optional)
  White and/or dark chocolate curls (optional)

1. In a large mixing bowl, combine sour cream, cream cheese, sugar, milk, and vanilla. Beat with an electric mixer on high speed until smooth.

2. In a small bowl, combine the ½ cup coffee and the coffee liqueur.

3. In a 2-quart rectangular dish, layer 1 package of the ladyfingers, cut sides up. Brush with half of the coffee mixture. Spread with half of the cream cheese mixture. Repeat with remaining ladyfingers, coffee mixture, and cream cheese mixture. Sprinkle with the 2 tablespoons cocoa powder. Cover and chill for 4 to 24 hours.

4. To serve, cut dessert into squares; arrange on a platter. If desired, sprinkle with additional unsweetened cocoa powder and garnish with white and/or dark chocolate curls. Makes 15 servings.

Cherry-Chocolate Bread Pudding

Whole grain bread adds heartiness to our upscale version of a humble dessert.

PER SERVING: 147 cal., 4 g total fat (2 g sat. fat), 1 mg chol., 152 mg sodium, 25 g carb., 3 g fiber, 7 g pro. Exchanges: 1.5 carb., 0.5 fat. Carb choices: 1.5.

  Nonstick cooking spray
- 2 cups firm-textured whole grain bread cubes (about 3 ounces)
- 3 tablespoons snipped dried tart red cherries
- 1 tablespoon toasted wheat germ
- ⅔ cup fat-free milk
- ¼ cup semisweet chocolate pieces
- ⅓ cup refrigerated or frozen egg product, thawed
- 1 teaspoon finely shredded orange peel
- ½ teaspoon vanilla
  Frozen light whipped dessert topping, thawed (optional)
  Unsweetened cocoa powder (optional)

1. Preheat oven to 350°F. Coat four 6-ounce individual soufflé dishes or custard cups with nonstick cooking spray. Divide bread cubes, cherries, and wheat germ among prepared dishes.

2. In a small saucepan, combine milk and chocolate. Cook and stir over low heat until the chocolate is melted; remove from heat. If necessary, beat smooth with a wire whisk.

3. In a small bowl, gradually stir chocolate mixture into egg. Stir in orange peel and vanilla. Pour mixture over bread cubes in dishes. Use the back of a spoon to press lightly to moisten bread.

4. Bake for 15 to 20 minutes or until tops appear firm and a knife inserted near centers comes out clean.

5. Serve warm. If desired, top with dessert topping and cocoa powder. Makes 4 servings.

Make-Ahead Directions: Prepare as directed through Step 3. Cover and chill for up to 2 hours. Preheat oven to 350°F. Continue as directed in Steps 4 and 5.

Cherry-Chocolate Bread Pudding

Cinnamon Raisin
Apple Indian Pudding

Cinnamon Raisin Apple Indian Pudding

Serve this colonial favorite for dessert or breakfast.

PER SERVING: 128 cal., 1 g total fat, (0 g sat. fat), 37 mg chol., 148 mg sodium, 26 g carb., 2 g fiber, 5 g pro. Exchanges: 0.5 carb., 1 fruit, 0.5 fat-free milk. Carb choices: 2.

PER SERVING WITH SUBSTITUTE: same as above, except 110 cal., 21 g carb. Exchanges: 0 carb. Carb choices: 1.5.

     Nonstick cooking spray
 2   cups fat-free milk
⅓   cup yellow cornmeal
 2   tablespoons packed brown sugar or brown sugar substitute* equivalent to 2 tablespoons brown sugar
½   teaspoon ground cinnamon
¼   teaspoon salt
 1   egg
 2   medium cooking apples (such as Jonathan or Rome Beauty), cored and chopped
¼   cup raisins

1. Preheat oven to 350°F. Coat six 6-ounce custard cups with cooking spray; place in a shallow baking pan. Set aside.

2. In a medium saucepan, heat 1½ cups of the milk just until boiling. In a small bowl, combine cornmeal and remaining ½ cup milk; whisk into hot milk. Cook and stir until boiling. Reduce heat. Cook and stir for 5 to 7 minutes or until thick. Remove from heat. Stir in brown sugar, cinnamon, and salt.

3. In a large bowl, beat egg; slowly stir in hot mixture. Stir in apples and raisins. Divide apple mixture among prepared cups. Bake about 30 minutes or until a knife inserted in centers comes out clean. Cool slightly. Serve warm. Makes 6 servings.

*Sugar Substitutes: Choose from Sweet'N Low Brown or Sugar Twin Granulated Brown. Follow the package directions to use the product amount equivalent to 2 tablespoons sugar.

Creamy Lime Mousse

This dessert offers a light touch to a big holiday meal.

PER SERVING: 112 cal., 9 g total fat (2 g sat. fat), 0 mg chol., 106 mg sodium, 4 g carb., 0 g fiber, 3 g pro. Exchanges: 1.5 fat, 0.5 medium-fat meat. Carb choices: 0.

 1   4-serving-size package sugar-free lime-flavored gelatin
 1   cup boiling water
½   teaspoon finely shredded lime peel
 2   tablespoons lime juice
¾   cup Tofu Sour Cream (see below) or one 8-ounce carton light dairy sour cream
1⅓   cups frozen light whipped dessert topping, thawed
      Lime peel curls or lime slices (optional)

1. In a large bowl, combine gelatin and water; stir about 2 minutes or until gelatin is dissolved. Stir in lime peel and juice. Cool for 10 to 15 minutes or until cool but not set. Whisk in Tofu Sour Cream. Gently whisk in 1 cup dessert topping. Pour into six 6- to 8-ounce glasses.

2. Cover and chill for 2 to 24 hours or until set. Garnish each with a tablespoon of topping and, if desired, lime peel or slices. Makes 6 (about ½-cup) servings.

Tofu Sour Cream: In a blender, combine half of a 12.3-ounce package extra-firm silken-style tofu (fresh bean curd), patted dry with paper towels; 3 tablespoons cooking oil; 4 teaspoons lemon juice; ¼ teaspoon honey; and ⅛ teaspoon salt. Cover and blend on high speed until smooth and creamy, stopping to push mixture into blades as needed. Makes about ¾ cup.

(sugar swap)

Based on our Test Kitchen results, we make the following recommendations for using sugar substitutes:

1. **In baking, replace no more than half of the sugar** with a sugar substitute.
2. **Check baked foods 5 to 10 minutes earlier** because they may cook faster.
3. **Use a sugar substitute blend** for cakes and cookies.
4. **When food will be cooked for more than 30 minutes,** avoid using aspartame (Equal), which breaks down with prolonged heat.
5. **If using aspartame** (Equal), add it to hot mixtures after cooking.
6. **For yeast breads,** leave some sugar as food for the yeast.
7. **Baked products made with sweeteners may dry out faster;** wrap them tightly with plastic wrap.
8. **Refrigerate jams and jellies when sugar is not acting as a preservative** and expect a softer set.
9. **Weigh whether the savings in calories and carbohydrates** is worth the expense in dollars.
10. **Decide if flavor is more important** and whether you can splurge on the real thing.

Creamy Lime Mousse

Brown Rice Pudding

Add this treat to your dessert buffet.

PER SERVING: 129 cal., 1 g total fat (0 g sat. fat), 2 mg chol., 126 mg sodium, 26 g carb., 1 g fiber, 6 g pro. Exchanges: 0.5 fat-free milk, 0.5 carb., 1 starch. Carb choices: 2.
PER SERVING WITH SUBSTITUTE: same as above, except 106 cal., 20 g carb. Exchanges: 0 carb. Carb choices: 1.

Nonstick cooking spray
4 cups fat-free milk
¾ cup regular brown rice
¼ cup sugar or sugar substitute* equivalent to ¼ cup sugar
¼ teaspoon salt
Ground cinnamon
½ cup chopped almonds, toasted (optional)

1. Preheat oven to 350°F. Lightly coat a 2-quart baking dish with nonstick cooking spray. In the prepared dish, combine milk, *uncooked* rice, sugar, and salt.

2. Cover and bake about 2 hours or until rice is very tender, stirring occasionally (the liquid will not be completely absorbed). Let stand, covered, for 30 minutes (mixture will thicken while standing). Serve warm. Sprinkle each serving with cinnamon and, if desired, almonds. Makes 8 (about ⅓-cup) servings.

Brown Rice Pudding

*Sugar Substitutes: Choose from Splenda granular or Sweet'N Low bulk or packets. Follow package directions to use product amount equivalent to ¼ cup sugar.

Make-Ahead Directions: Prepare pudding as directed, except cover and chill for up to 24 hours before serving. If necessary, to thin, stir in 2 to 4 tablespoons fat-free milk.

Cranberry Poached Pears

When company's coming, serve these delicate double-cranberry pears as an elegant finale to dinner. (Pictured on page 5.)

PER SERVING: 103 cal., 1 g total fat (0 g sat. fat), 2 mg chol., 36 mg sodium, 24 g carb., 3 g fiber, 2 g pro. Exchanges: 1.5 fruit. Carb choices: 1.5.

2½ cups reduced-calorie cranberry juice
3 small pears, halved, peeled, and cored
1 vanilla bean,* halved lengthwise
2 3-inch-long cinnamon sticks
¼ teaspoon freshly ground black pepper
½ cup fresh cranberries
1 6-ounce carton plain low-fat yogurt
2 teaspoons honey

1. In a medium saucepan, bring cranberry juice to a simmer. Add pears, split vanilla bean, stick cinnamon, and pepper. Return to a simmer; cover and cook for 10 minutes. Remove from heat. Add cranberries. Let stand, covered, for 1 hour, turning pears once.

2. Remove vanilla bean and scrape seeds into a small bowl; stir in yogurt and honey.

3. Divide cooking liquid among six individual dessert dishes. Add a pear half to each. Top with yogurt mixture. Makes 6 servings.

*Test Kitchen Tip: Instead of using a vanilla bean, you can add 1 teaspoon vanilla to the cooking liquid before letting the mixture stand and stir ½ teaspoon vanilla into the yogurt mixture.

Make-Ahead Directions: Prepare as directed through Step 2. Place pears and the cooking liquid in an airtight container. Place yogurt mixture in another airtight container. Cover and chill for up to 24 hours. Serve as directed in Step 3.

Lemon Soufflé Dessert

If you use sugar substitute, expect a browner top.

PER SERVING: 190 cal., 5 g total fat (3 g sat. fat), 111 mg chol., 92 mg sodium, 29 g carb., 0 g fiber, 7 g pro. Exchanges: 2 carb., 0.5 medium-fat meat, 0.5 fat. Carb choices: 2.

PER SERVING WITH SUBSTITUTE: same as above, except 156 cal., 20 g carb. Exchanges: 1.5 carb. Carb choices: 1.

Nonstick cooking spray
6 tablespoons granulated sugar or sugar-substitute blend* equivalent to 6 tablespoons sugar
¼ cup all-purpose flour
2 teaspoons finely shredded lemon peel
¼ cup lemon juice
1 tablespoon butter, melted
2 egg yolks
1 cup fat-free milk
3 egg whites
   Sifted powdered sugar

1. Preheat oven to 350°F. Spray a 1-quart soufflé dish with nonstick cooking spray. In a large bowl, combine 2 tablespoons sugar and flour; whisk in peel, juice, and butter until smooth. In a small bowl, whisk together yolks and milk; whisk into lemon mixture. Set aside.

2. In a mixing bowl, beat egg whites with an electric mixer on medium speed until soft peaks form (tips curl). Slowly add 4 tablespoons of the granulated sugar, beating on high speed until stiff peaks form (tips stand straight). Fold a small amount of whites into lemon mixture. Fold in the remaining egg whites (batter will be thin).

3. Pour batter into soufflé dish; place in a pan. Place on oven rack; pour boiling water into pan around dish to a depth of 1 inch. Bake, uncovered, about 40 minutes or until the top springs back when lightly touched. Cool for 5 minutes on a rack. Top with powdered sugar. Serve warm. Makes 4 servings.

*Sugar Substitutes: Choose from Splenda Sugar Blend for Baking or Equal Sugar Lite. Follow directions to use product amount equivalent to 6 tablespoons sugar.

Mocha Cream Puffs

(the sweet truth)

A healthful meal plan for people with diabetes can include some sugar. That's a good thing because sugar plays an important role in baking. Besides adding sweetness, sugar adds shape and structure and contributes to browning and tenderness in baked foods such as cakes. Another good thing: Some of our recipes allow for sugar substitutes and blends that retain sweetness and save on calories. For more on sugar and substitutes, see "Sugar Swap," page 139, and "How Sweet It Is," page 152.

Mocha Cream Puffs

These light-as-air puffs can be made, covered, and stored at room temperature for up to 24 hours before filling. The filling can be prepared and chilled up to 2 hours ahead.

PER PUFF: 63 cal., 3 g total fat (2 g sat. fat), 37 mg chol., 42 mg sodium, 6 g carb., 0 g fiber, 2 g pro. Exchanges: 0.5 carb., 0.5 fat. Carb choices: 0.5.

Nonstick cooking spray
- ¾ cup water
- 3 tablespoons butter
- 1 teaspoon instant coffee crystals
- ⅛ teaspoon salt
- ¾ cup all-purpose flour
- 3 eggs
- 1 recipe Mocha Filling (see below)

1. Preheat oven to 400°F. Coat a very large baking sheet with cooking spray; set aside.

2. In a saucepan, combine water, butter, coffee crystals, and salt. Bring to boiling. Add flour all at once, stirring vigorously. Cook and stir until a ball forms that doesn't separate. Cool for 5 minutes.

3. Add eggs, 1 at a time, beating with a wooden spoon after each addition until smooth. Drop into 20 small mounds onto prepared baking sheet. Bake about 25 minutes or until brown. Cool on a wire rack. Split puffs; remove soft dough from insides.

4. Using a pastry bag fitted with a star tip or a spoon, pipe or spoon Mocha Filling into cream puff bottoms. Add cream puff tops. Makes 20 puffs.

Mocha Filling: In a medium bowl, combine ½ cup low-fat vanilla yogurt, 2 tablespoons unsweetened cocoa powder, and 1 teaspoon instant coffee crystals. Fold in half of an 8-ounce container light whipped dessert topping, thawed. Cover and chill filling up to 2 hours.

Apple-Mango Crisp

Fresh mango is often available, but if you can't find it, look for the refrigerated variety in a jar in the produce section.

PER SERVING: 164 cal., 6 g total fat (2 g sat. fat), 8 mg chol., 2 mg sodium, 28 g carb., 3 g fiber, 3 g pro. Exchanges: 0.5 starch, 0.5 carb., 1 fruit, 1 fat. Carb choices: 2.

PER SERVING WITH SUBSTITUTE: same as above, except 138 cal., 21 g carb. Exchanges: 0 carb. Carb choices: 1.5.

Nonstick cooking spray
- ¾ cup all-purpose flour
- ¾ cup rolled oats
- ½ cup toasted wheat germ
- ½ cup packed brown sugar or brown sugar substitute* equivalent to ½ cup brown sugar
- 1½ teaspoons ground cinnamon
- ¼ cup butter, melted
- 4 green cooking apples (such as Granny Smith)
- 2 red cooking apples (such as Gala, Rome Beauty, or Fuji), cored and chopped
- 3 tablespoons lime juice
- 2 medium mangoes, pitted, peeled, and chopped
- ⅓ cup chopped pecans
  Frozen light whipped dessert topping, thawed (optional)

1. Preheat oven to 375°F. Coat two 1½- or 2-quart baking dishes or a 3-quart rectangular baking dish with nonstick cooking spray.

2. For topping, in a medium bowl, stir together ½ cup of the flour, the oats, wheat germ, brown sugar, and cinnamon. Stir in butter; set aside.

3. Place apples in a very large bowl. Stir in lime juice. Stir in remaining ¼ cup flour. Fold in mangoes.

4. Place apple-mango mixture in prepared baking dish(es). Top with oat topping. Bake, uncovered, for 30 minutes. Sprinkle with pecans; bake for 10 to 15 minutes more or until apples are tender.

5. Cool slightly. Serve warm. If desired, top with dessert topping. Makes 16 (¾-cup) servings.

*Sugar Substitutes: Choose from Sweet'N Low Brown or Sugar Twin Granulated Brown. Follow the package directions to use amount equivalent to ½ cup brown sugar.

Apple-Mango Crisp

Devil's Food Ice Cream Pie

Mini Cranberry Phyllo Tarts

Short on time? Substitute a 2.1-ounce package baked miniature phyllo dough shells (15) for the phyllo tart shells. Prepare as directed, starting with Step 6.

PER TART: 29 cal., 0 g total fat (0 g sat. fat), 0 mg chol., 17 mg sodium, 6 g carb., 0 g fiber, 0 g pro. Exchanges: 0.5 carb. Carb choices: 0.5.

Nonstick cooking spray
4 sheets frozen phyllo dough (14×9-inch rectangles), thawed
¾ cup fresh cranberries
½ cup water
1 tablespoon sugar
⅓ cup canned whole cranberry sauce
⅓ cup lemon fat-free yogurt
3 tablespoons frozen light whipped dessert topping, thawed
Fresh mint leaves (optional)

1. Preheat oven to 350°F. Coat twelve 1¾-inch muffin cups with nonstick cooking spray; set aside.

2. Unfold phyllo dough. Remove one sheet of the phyllo dough; lightly coat phyllo sheet with nonstick cooking spray. Working quickly, top with the remaining phyllo sheets, coating each sheet with nonstick cooking spray.

3. Cut phyllo stack lengthwise into three 3-inch-wide strips. Cut each strip crosswise into five 2¾×3-inch rectangles, making 15 rectangles total.

4. For tart shells, press each phyllo rectangle into a prepared muffin cup, pleating edges as needed to fit. Bake about 8 minutes or until golden.

5. Cool phyllo tart shells in muffin cups on a wire rack for 5 minutes. Carefully remove tart shells from muffin cups; cool on a wire rack.

6. Meanwhile, for topping, in a small saucepan, combine cranberries, the water, and sugar. Cook and stir over medium heat until boiling. Reduce heat; simmer, uncovered, for 1 minute.

7. Remove from heat. Cool cranberries for 15 minutes. Drain and discard the cooking liquid. Place cranberries in a small bowl; cover and chill for 4 hours.

8. For filling, in a small bowl, stir cranberry sauce to break up. In another small bowl, fold together yogurt and whipped dessert topping.

9. Just before serving, place 1 teaspoon of the cranberry sauce filling into each phyllo tart shell. Divide yogurt mixture among tarts. Top each tart with about 3 chilled cooked cranberries. If desired, garnish with fresh mint leaves. Makes 15 tarts.

Make-Ahead Directions: Prepare phyllo tart shells as directed through Step 5. Place phyllo shells in a single layer in an airtight container; store at room temperature for up to 2 days. Prepare the cranberry topping as directed in Steps 6 and 7; cover and chill for up to 2 days. Continue as directed in Steps 8 and 9.

Devil's Food Ice Cream Pie

Add the chocolate syrup after freezing the pie—otherwise, the chocolate flavor won't be as strong.

PER SERVING: 192 cal., 6 g total fat (3 g sat. fat), 16 mg chol., 132 mg sodium, 34 g carb., 1 g fiber, 5 g pro. Exchanges: 2.5 carb., 0.5 Fat. Carb choices: 2.5.

1 6¾-oz. box low-fat devil's food cookie cakes (12 cookies)
¼ cup reduced-fat peanut butter
¼ cup hot water
1 cup sliced bananas
4 cups no-sugar-added light vanilla ice cream, softened
2 tablespoons chocolate-flavored syrup

1. Coarsely chop cookie cakes. Place cookie pieces in the bottom of an 8-inch springform pan.

2. In a small bowl, whisk together peanut butter and the hot water until smooth. Drizzle evenly over cookies.

3. Top with banana slices and carefully spoon ice cream evenly over all. Spread ice cream on top until smooth. Cover with plastic wrap and place in freezer until firm, about 8 hours.

4. Let stand at room temperature for 15 minutes before serving. Remove the sides of the pan; drizzle chocolate syrup over all. Makes 10 servings.

(ode to pumpkin)

The humble pumpkin deserves some respect. Not only is pumpkin delicious in pies, muffins, breads, and soups, but it is also a nutritional powerhouse. For starters, pumpkin is packed with beta-carotene, a potent antioxidant. It's also a terrific source of fiber. A half cup of canned pumpkin contains 5 grams of fiber. Yet it has only about 40 calories and 0.5 gram of fat, while providing small amounts of vitamins and minerals. So go ahead. Try one—or all three—of our pumpkin desserts.

Light and Luscious Pumpkin Pie

Everyone will give thanks for this streamlined pie—just as satisfying as the original.

PER SERVING: 195 cal., 8 g total fat (1 g sat. fat), 1 mg chol., 108 mg sodium, 28 g carb., 2 g fiber, 5 g pro. Exchanges: 0.5 starch, 1.5 carb., 1 fat. Carb choices: 2.

PER SERVING WITH SUBSTITUTE: same as above, except 171 cal., 22 g carb. Exchanges: 1 carb. Carb choices: 1.5.

- 1 recipe Oil Pastry (see right)
- ½ cup refrigerated or frozen egg product, thawed, or 2 eggs
- 1 15-ounce can pumpkin
- ⅓ cup sugar or sugar substitute* equivalent to ⅓ cup sugar
- 2 tablespoons honey
- 1 teaspoon ground cinnamon
- 1 teaspoon vanilla
- ¼ teaspoon ground ginger
- ¼ teaspoon ground nutmeg
- ¾ cup evaporated fat-free milk
  Frozen fat-free whipped dessert topping, thawed (optional)

Light and Luscious Pumpkin Pie

1. Preheat oven to 450°F. On a well-floured surface, flatten Oil Pastry. Roll dough from center to edge into a round about 12 inches in diameter.

2. Wrap pastry around rolling pin; unroll into a 9-inch pie plate. Ease pastry into plate, being careful not to stretch. Trim to ½ inch beyond edge of pie plate. Fold under extra pastry. Flute or crimp edge as desired. Do not prick shell. Line pastry with a double thickness of heavy foil. Bake for 8 minutes. Remove foil. Bake for 5 minutes more. Cool on a wire rack.

3. Set oven temperature to 375°F. In a bowl, beat egg; stir in pumpkin, sugar, honey, cinnamon, vanilla, ginger, and nutmeg. Beat just until combined. Slowly stir in milk. Pour into pastry shell. To prevent overbrowning, cover edge of pie with foil.

4. Bake for 40 to 45 minutes or until filling appears set (edges of filling may crack slightly). Cool on a wire rack for 1 hour. Cover and chill for at least 2 hours. If desired, serve with dessert topping. Makes 10 servings.

Oil Pastry: In a medium bowl, stir together 1⅓ cups all-purpose flour and ¼ teaspoon salt. Add ⅓ cup cooking oil and 3 tablespoons fat-free milk all at once to flour mixture. Stir lightly with a fork. Form into a ball.

*Sugar Substitutes: Choose from Splenda granular or Sweet'N Low bulk or packets. Follow the package directions to use the product amount equivalent to ⅓ cup sugar.

Raisin-Pumpkin Tart

If you like, make this two-layer tart more elegant
with fat-free whipped dessert topping.

PER SERVING: 229 cal., 13 g total fat (4 g sat. fat), 49 mg chol., 151 mg
sodium, 23 g carb., 1 g fiber, 6 g pro. Exchanges: 0.5 starch, 1 carb.,
0.5 medium-fat meat, 2 fat. Carb choices: 1.5.
PER SERVING WITH SUBSTITUTE: same as above, except 214 cal.,
19 g carb. Exchanges: 0.5 carb. Carb choices: 1.

- 1 recipe **Oil Pastry** (see recipe, page 145)
- 1 8-ounce package reduced-fat cream cheese
  (Neufchâtel), softened
- 1 egg yolk
- 1 tablespoon honey
- ¼ cup sliced almonds, toasted and finely chopped
- ¼ cup golden raisins, snipped
- 1 cup canned pumpkin
- 1 5-ounce can (⅔ cup) evaporated fat-free milk
- ¼ cup sugar or sugar substitute* equivalent to
  ¼ cup sugar
- 1 egg
- 1 egg white
- 2 teaspoons pumpkin pie spice
- 2 tablespoons sliced almonds, toasted (optional)

146 DIABETIC LIVING | HOLIDAY COOKING

1. Preheat oven to 450°F. Prepare Oil Pastry. On a well-floured surface, slightly flatten dough. Roll pastry from center to edge into a 12-inch round.

2. To transfer, wrap pastry around rolling pin. Unroll pastry into a 10-inch tart pan with a removable bottom. Ease pastry into pan, being careful not to stretch pastry. Press edge of pastry against edge of pan. Trim edges. Do not prick shell. Line pastry with a double thickness of heavy foil. Bake for 8 minutes. Remove foil. Bake for 4 to 5 minutes more or until golden.

3. Meanwhile, for cream cheese layer, in a medium mixing bowl, combine cream cheese, egg yolk, and honey; beat with an electric mixer on low to medium speed until combined. Stir in chopped almonds and raisins; set mixture aside.

4. For pumpkin layer, in another medium bowl, stir together pumpkin, evaporated milk, sugar, whole egg, egg white, and pumpkin pie spice; set aside.

5. Reduce oven temperature to 375°F. Carefully spoon cream cheese filling into hot baked pastry; spread evenly. Pour pumpkin mixture over cream cheese layer; spread evenly.

6. Bake for 30 to 35 minutes or until set. Cool on a wire rack for 1 hour. Cover and chill for at least 2 hours.

7. To serve, remove side of pan; using a large spatula, carefully lift tart from pan bottom and slide onto a platter. If desired, garnish with sliced almonds. Makes 12 servings.

*Sugar Substitutes: Choose from Splenda granular, Equal Spoonful or packets, or Sweet'N Low bulk or packets. Follow the package directions to use the product amount equivalent to 1/4 cup sugar.

No-Bake Pumpkin Swirl Cheesecake

A narrow, thin-bladed spatula or a table knife works best for swirling the batter.

PER SERVING: 179 cal., 7 g total fat (4 g sat. fat), 23 mg chol., 331 mg sodium, 19 g carb., 1 g fiber, 9 g pro. Exchanges: 1 carb., 1.5 fat. Carb choices: 1.

PER SERVING WITH SUGAR SUBSTITUTE: same as above, except 149 cal., 10 g carb.

- ¾ cup finely crushed graham crackers
- 2 tablespoons butter, melted
- 1 8-ounce package reduced-fat cream cheese (Neufchâtel)
- ½ cup sugar or sugar substitute* equivalent to ½ cup sugar
- ½ cup fat-free milk
- 2 teaspoons vanilla
- ½ teaspoon finely shredded orange peel
- 2 8-ounce packages fat-free cream cheese
- 1 15-ounce can pumpkin
- 1 teaspoon pumpkin pie spice
- 1 envelope unflavored gelatin
- ¼ cup orange juice

1. For crust, in a bowl, combine graham cracker crumbs and melted butter; stir until crumbs are moistened. Press onto bottom of an 8-inch springform pan. Cover; chill.

2. For white filling, in a food processor, combine the reduced-fat cream cheese, 1/4 cup of the sugar, 1/4 cup of the milk, the vanilla, and peel. Cover; process until smooth. Transfer to a bowl; set aside.

3. For pumpkin filling, in a food processor, combine the fat-free cream cheese, pumpkin, remaining 1/4 cup sugar, remaining 1/4 cup milk, and the pumpkin pie spice. Cover; process until smooth.

4. In a small saucepan, sprinkle gelatin over juice; let stand for 5 minutes. Cook and stir over low heat until gelatin is dissolved. Stir 1 tablespoon gelatin mixture into white filling; stir remaining gelatin into pumpkin filling.

5. Pour pumpkin filling into crust. Carefully pour white filling onto pumpkin filling. Use a knife to swirl pumpkin and white mixtures. Cover and chill overnight. To serve, loosen cheesecake from side of pan; remove side of pan. Cut into wedges. Makes 12 servings.

*Sugar Substitutes: Choose from Splenda Granular, Equal Spoonful or packets, or Sweet'N Low bulk or packets. Follow package directions to use the product amount equivalent to 1/2 cup sugar.

Orange-Cranberry Cake

Cranberries add a merry accent and tangy flavor in addition to powerful antioxidants to this cake.

PER SERVING: 187 cal., 4 g total fat (2 g sat. fat), 44 mg chol., 122 mg sodium, 34 g carb., 1 g fiber, 4 g pro. Exchanges: 1 starch, 1.5 carb., 0.5 fat. Carb choices: 2.

PER SERVING WITH SUBSTITUTE: same as above, except 165 cal., 26 g carb. Exchanges: 1 starch, 1 carb. Carb choices: 2.

Nonstick cooking spray
2 cups all-purpose flour
1¼ teaspoons baking powder
½ teaspoon baking soda
3 tablespoons butter, softened
1 cup granulated sugar or sugar substitute baking blend* equivalent to 1 cup sugar
2 eggs
⅔ cup plain fat-free yogurt
2 cups fresh cranberries, chopped
1 teaspoon finely shredded orange peel
Sifted powdered sugar (optional)

1. Preheat oven to 350°F. Coat a 10-inch fluted tube pan with nonstick cooking spray; set aside. In a medium bowl, stir together flour, baking powder, and baking soda; set aside.

2. In a large mixing bowl, beat butter with an electric mixer on medium speed for 30 seconds. Add granulated sugar; beat until fluffy. Add eggs, 1 at a time, beating well after each addition. Alternately add flour mixture and yogurt to egg mixture, beating after each addition just until combined. Fold in cranberries and peel.

3. Spoon batter into prepared pan; spread evenly. Bake about 40 minutes or until a toothpick inserted near the center comes out clean.

4. Cool in pan on a wire rack for 10 minutes. Remove from pan. Cool completely on a wire rack. If desired, sprinkle with powdered sugar. Makes 12 servings.

*Sugar Substitutes: If using a substitute, add ¼ cup water to yogurt before adding to egg mixture. Choose from Splenda Sugar Blend for Baking or Equal Sugar Lite. Follow the package directions to use the product amount equivalent to 1 cup sugar.

Apple Cake with Hot Coconut-Brown Sugar Topping

Leave on the apple peels for added fiber, nutrients, and, of course, ease. Young guests will love this cake.

PER SERVING: 186 cal., 9 g total fat (4 g sat. fat), 19 mg chol., 112 mg sodium, 26 g carb., 2 g fiber, 2 g pro. Exchanges: 1.5 carb., 2 fat. Carb choices: 2.

PER SERVING SUBSTITUTE: same as above, except 164 cal., 19 g carb. Exchanges: 1 carb. Carb choices: 1.

Nonstick cooking spray
¾ cup granulated sugar or sugar substitute blend* equivalent to ¾ cup granulated sugar
½ cup vanilla fat-free yogurt
¼ cup cooking oil
1 egg or ¼ cup refrigerated or frozen egg product, thawed
1½ teaspoons ground cinnamon
1 teaspoon vanilla
½ teaspoon baking powder
¼ teaspoon salt
¼ teaspoon baking soda
¼ teaspoon ground ginger
¼ teaspoon ground nutmeg
1¼ cups all-purpose flour
1 pound green cooking apples (such as Granny Smith or Crispin), cored and coarsely chopped (3 cups)
1 cup flaked coconut
3 tablespoons butter
3 tablespoons packed brown sugar or brown sugar substitute* equivalent to 3 tablespoons brown sugar
2 tablespoons fat-free milk

Orange-Cranberry Cake

Apple Cake with Hot Coconut-Brown Sugar Topping

1. Preheat oven to 325°F. Line two 8×4×2-inch loaf pans with foil; lightly coat foil with nonstick cooking spray. Set aside.

2. In a large bowl, stir together granulated sugar, yogurt, oil, egg, 1 teaspoon of the cinnamon, the vanilla, baking powder, salt, baking soda, ginger, and nutmeg. Stir in flour just until combined. Fold in apples (the batter will be thick and chunky).

3. Spoon batter into prepared pans; spread evenly. Bake about 45 minutes or until a toothpick inserted near centers comes out clean and tops are brown.

4. Meanwhile, for topping, in a small saucepan, combine coconut, butter, brown sugar, milk, and remaining ½ teaspoon cinnamon. Cook and stir over low heat until the butter is melted.

5. Preheat the broiler. Gently spread topping evenly onto cakes. Broil 4 inches from heat for 2 to 3 minutes or until topping is bubbly and light brown.

6. Cool cakes in pans on wire racks for 45 minutes. Use foil to lift cakes from pans; remove foil. Serve warm or cool. Makes 2 cakes (16 servings total).

*Sugar Substitutes: For cake, choose from Splenda Sugar Blend for Baking or Equal Sugar Lite. Follow the package directions to use the product amount that's equivalent to ¾ cup granulated sugar. For topping, choose from Sweet'N Low Brown or Sugar Twin Granulated Brown. Follow the package directions to use product amount equivalent to 3 tablespoons brown sugar.

Make-Ahead Directions: Prepare as directed; cool. Wrap and store in the refrigerator for up to 3 days.

managing your diabetes

Understanding diabetes gives you a better chance of controlling it and preventing complications. It pays to learn all you can, then develop a plan that fits your lifestyle.

An estimated 21 million people in the United States, or 7 percent of the U.S. population, have diabetes, according to the Centers for Disease Control and Prevention. An additional 54 million Americans have pre-diabetes—indicating an increased risk of developing diabetes. If you're one of them, remember that you—not your doctor, dietitian, or other health professional—play the most important role in staying healthy.

Define Your Diabetes

Your health-care team will work with you to develop a personalized diabetes management plan, consisting of healthful foods, physical activity, and, if necessary, the medication that's right for you and your type of diabetes (type 1, type 2, or gestational).

Type 1 diabetes: In this type, the pancreas doesn't produce insulin, so people with type 1 diabetes must take insulin. A typical treatment plan begins with an individualized meal plan, guidelines for physical activity, and blood glucose testing. Insulin therapy is then planned around lifestyle and eating patterns.

Type 2 diabetes: In type 2 diabetes, either the pancreas doesn't produce enough insulin or the body doesn't properly respond to insulin, so too much glucose remains in the blood. Many people control type 2 diabetes by following a specially designed meal plan and engaging in regular physical activity. The right plan can help people reach and attain a desirable weight, plus healthy blood glucose, blood cholesterol, and blood pressure levels. As the disease progresses, treatment may expand to include oral medications, oral medications with insulin, or insulin alone.

Gestational diabetes: This type develops only during pregnancy. Women who've had gestational diabetes have a higher risk of developing type 2 diabetes.

Develop Your Meal Plan

Adhering to a healthful meal plan is one of the most important measures you can take to control your blood glucose. Work with a dietitian to design a meal plan that reflects your individual needs and preferences. Your meal plan should also:

* Include fruits, vegetables, and whole grains.
* Reduce the amount of saturated fat and cholesterol you eat.
* Minimize the amount of salt or sodium you eat.
* Incorporate a moderate amount of sugar because some sugar can be part of a healthful diabetes meal plan.
* Help you maintain or achieve an ideal weight.

Follow Your Meal Plan

As you start following your meal plan, you'll see that it gives you some flexibility regarding what, how much, and when you eat, but you have to be comfortable with the foods it suggests. It will guide you in eating appropriate amounts of three major nutrients—carbohydrates, protein, and fat—at the right times. Your meal plan will be nutritionally balanced, allowing you to get the vitamins, minerals, and fiber your body needs. And if you need to lose weight, it will indicate how many calories you should consume every day in order to lose the extra pounds at a realistic pace.

Your meal plan can be simple, especially if you use a proven technique to keep track of what you're eating. Two well-known meal-planning systems for diabetes are diabetic exchanges and carbohydrate counting. Your dietitian may suggest one or the other. To help you follow either system, every recipe in this book provides nutrition information, including the number of exchanges and carb choices in each serving. (Turn to page 153 to see how to use this information.)

Track the Exchanges

Exchange Lists for Meal Planning outlines a system designed by the American Diabetes Association and the American Dietetic Association. To use the exchange system, your dietitian will work with you to develop a pattern of food exchanges—or a meal plan— suited to your specific needs. You'll be able to keep track of the number of exchanges from various food groups that you eat each day. Tally those numbers and match the total

to the daily allowance set in your meal plan. (For more information, see www.diabetes.org.)

Count Carbohydrates

Carbohydrate counting is the method many diabetes educators prefer for keeping tabs on what you eat. It makes sense because the carbohydrate content of foods has the greatest effect on blood glucose levels. If you focus on carbohydrates, you can eat a variety of foods and still control your blood glucose.

When counting carbohydrates, you can tally the number of grams you eat each day. Or you can count the number of carbohydrate choices, which allows you to work with smaller numbers. We offer both numbers with our recipes.

(**monitor your blood glucose**)

Whether you have type 1 or type 2 diabetes, it's important to test your blood glucose, especially if you're taking insulin shots or oral medication. Usually you test blood glucose before each meal. Your health-care providers will teach you how to measure your blood glucose with a simple finger-prick test, as well as how to adjust your food intake, physical activity, and/or medication when your blood glucose is too high or too low. Your health-care providers will help you set blood glucose goals. For example, the American Diabetes Association suggests a target for fasting or before meals is 90 to 130 milligrams/deciliter. At two hours after the start of a meal, the goal is less than 180 milligrams/deciliter. Your A1C level (the average amount of glucose in the blood over the last few months) should be less than 7. To keep your blood glucose at a healthy level, follow these five important guidelines:

* Eat about the same amount of food each day.
* Eat meals and snacks at about the same times each day.
* Do not skip meals or snacks.
* Take medicines at the same times each day.
* Do physical activity at about the same times each day.

(**low-calorie sweeteners**)

There's no need to dump low-calorie sweeteners just because sugar is safer than once thought. Sweeteners are "free foods" in your meal plan—and that's a good thing! They make foods taste sweet, they have no calories, and they won't raise your blood glucose levels. The following sweeteners are accepted by the Food and Drug Administration as safe to eat: aspartame (Equal and NutraSweet), acesulfame potassium (Sweet One), saccharin (Sweet'N Low and Sugar Twin), and sucralose (Splenda).

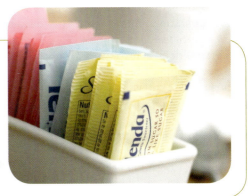

Basic carbohydrate counting relies on eating about the same amount of carbohydrates at the same times each day to keep blood glucose levels in your target range. It's a good meal-planning method if you have type 2 diabetes and take no daily oral diabetes medications or take one to two shots of insulin per day.

Advanced carbohydrate counting is a more complex method than the basic system of carbohydrate counting. It's designed for individuals who take multiple daily insulin injections or use an insulin pump. With advanced carbohydrate counting, you have to balance the amount of carbohydrates you consume with the insulin you take. You estimate the amount of carbohydrates you'll be eating and adjust your mealtime insulin dose based on your recommended insulin-to-carbohydrate ratio. To learn how to follow advanced carbohydrate counting, seek the assistance of a registered dietitian or certified diabetes educator.

The Carbohydrate Question
Although the calories from fat, protein, and carbohydrates all affect your blood glucose level, carbohydrates affect it the most. So why not just avoid carbohydrates altogether? While carbohydrates may be the main nutrient that raises blood glucose levels, you shouldn't cut them from your diet. Foods that contain carbohydrates are among the most healthful available—vegetables, fruits, whole grains, and low- or nonfat dairy foods. Eliminating these foods could compromise your health.

(be a sugar sleuth)

Knowing the different forms of sugar can make life sweeter when you're reading labels and recipes. Sugar content is included in the total grams we list for carbohydrates in recipes.

* Sucrose appears in table sugar, molasses, beet sugar, brown sugar, cane sugar, powdered sugar, raw sugar, turbinado, and maple syrup.
* Other "-ose" sugars include glucose (or dextrose), fructose, lactose, and maltose. Fructose and sugar alcohols affect blood glucose less than sucrose, but large amounts of fructose may increase blood fat levels.
* Sugar alcohols such as sorbitol, xylitol, maltitol, mannitol, lactitol, and erythritol should only be eaten in moderation because they can cause diarrhea, gas, and cramping.

How Sweet It Is
For many years, people with diabetes were told to shun sugar because it was thought that sugar caused blood glucose to soar out of control. So they diligently wiped sugary foods and sugar out of their diets, hoping to stabilize their blood glucose levels. Today, more than a dozen studies have shown sugars in foods don't cause blood glucose to spike any higher or faster than starches, such as those in potatoes and bread. The American Diabetes Association's recommendations on sugar now state "scientific evidence has shown that the use of sucrose (table sugar) as part of the meal plan does not impair blood glucose control in individuals with type 1 or type 2 diabetes."

It is important to note, however, that sugar is not a "free food." It still contains calories and offers no nutritional value beyond providing energy. So when you eat foods that contain sugar, they have to replace other carbohydrate-rich foods in your meal plan. Carbohydrates you eat contain a healthful amount of vitamins, minerals, and fiber. So it's a good idea to focus on whole grains and vegetables for your carbohydrates rather than sugar. Talk to your dietitian to determine a healthful way to include a moderate amount of sugar in your meal plan. Or you can also sweeten foods with sugar substitutes (see "Low-Calorie Sweeteners," page 151).

Stay Involved and Informed
Eating healthfully, exercising, and monitoring blood glucose levels help keep diabetes in check—all easier to do if you follow the plans you've developed with your health-care providers. Update them on your progress and request changes if something isn't working. And stay informed about diabetes by going to www.diabeticlivingonline.com to sign up for our e-mail newsletter. You're the one who can monitor your progress day by day.

(using our nutrition information)

At the top of every one of our recipes, you'll see the nutrition information listed for each serving. You'll find the amount of calories (cal.), total fat, saturated fat (sat. fat), cholesterol (chol.), sodium, total carbohydrates (carb.), fiber, and protein (pro.). In addition, you'll find the number of diabetic exchanges for each serving and the number of carbohydrate choices, in case you prefer those methods to keep track of what you're eating.

PER SERVING: 134 cal., 9 g total fat (1 g sat. fat), 0 mg chol., 60 mg sodium, 14 g carb., 4 g fiber, 2 g pro. Exchanges: 0.5 fruit, 1 vegetable, 2 fat. Carb choices: 1.

Interpreting the Numbers
Use our nutrition analyses to keep track of the nutritional value of the foods you eat, following the meal plan you and your dietitian have decided is right for you. Refer to that plan to see how a recipe fits the number of diabetic exchanges or carbohydrate choices you're allotted for each day. When

you try a recipe, jot down our nutrition numbers to keep a running tally of what you're eating, remembering your daily allowances. At the end of each day, see how your numbers compare to your plan.

Diabetic Exchanges
The exchange system allows you to choose from a variety of items within several food groupings. Those groupings include starch, fruit, fat-free milk, carbohydrates, nonstarchy vegetables, meat and meat substitutes, fat, and free foods. To use the diabetic exchange system with our recipes, follow your plan's recommendations on the number of servings you should select from each exchange group in a day.

Carbohydrate Counting
Our recipes help you keep track of carbohydrates in two ways—tallying grams of carbohydrates and the number of carbohydrate choices. For counting grams, add the amounts of total carbohydrates to your running total for the day. For carbohydrate choices,

one choice equals 15 grams of carbohydrates. For example, a sandwich made with two slices of bread is 2 carbohydrate choices. The benefit of this system is that you're keeping track of small numbers.

Calculating Method
To calculate our nutrition information and offer flexibility in our recipes, we've made some decisions about what's included in our analyses and what's not. We follow these guidelines when we analyze recipes that list ingredient options or serving suggestions:

* When ingredient choices appear (such as yogurt or sour cream), we use the first one mentioned for the analysis.
* When an ingredient is listed as optional, such as a garnish or a suggested serve-along, we don't include it in our nutrition analysis.
* When we offer a range in the number of servings, we use the smaller number.
* For marinades, we assume most of it is discarded.

dining out
during the holidays

The holidays often bring with them invitations to parties held at restaurants. While these gatherings can be fun, learning to strike a balance between pleasure and health is essential if you have diabetes.

Dining out healthfully is no simple feat any time of year. It's difficult enough to plan and prepare balanced meals at home. But when faced with mouthwatering images, enticing descriptions, and the persuasion of a server or dining companion, even the most disciplined eater may fall victim to the menu's allure. Many people feel dining out is a special occasion and throw all caution to the wind. However, since the average American eats four or more meals away from home each week, this approach is not the best.

Monitor Your Portions
Restaurants serve too much food. You're probably used to seeing gargantuan servings of pasta, salad, Mexican foods, and meat. In fact, most dishes could easily serve two to four people based on recommended

serving sizes. Customers must take it upon themselves to modify eating behaviors. Here are a few suggestions: Order less food, stop eating when you're no longer hungry (not stuffed full), request to-go containers, and learn to share with a dining companion.

Common Snags

Most restaurant foods are higher in fat and sodium than recipes prepared at home. Since customers cannot supervise a chef's cooking practices, there is no way to know how much fat or salt he or she is adding to the food. These extra ingredients are not typically clarified on the menu. When you're trying to limit sodium and fat intake, your only ammunition is to inquire about the cooking and seasoning methods when ordering and make special requests, as appropriate. For example, request that your stir-fry be lightly sautéed or that your meat be cooked plain, without added seasoning salts or butter.

You Are In Control

Making good choices when dining out can be challenging, but restaurants are ultimately there to please you—the customer. You have the power to order healthful foods and the freedom to make special requests. Following the 12 practical tips at right will help you celebrate the season and still maintain blood glucose control, boost nutrition, and improve your health.

(12 dining-out tips)

1. **When ordering an entrée,** look for the words grilled, baked, steamed, broiled, roasted, and poached. Be aware of terms that signal high fat content: fried, breaded, creamed, battered, scalloped, pan-fried, crispy, flaky, and buttered.
2. **Always ask for** dressings, sauces, and gravies on the side and use these sparingly.
3. **When choosing side dishes,** stick to steamed or lightly sautéed vegetables, fresh fruit, a plain baked potato, cottage cheese, applesauce, low-fat beans, or a side salad. Baked potatoes are often large; eat only half and don't add the extra toppings, such as butter, sour cream, and bacon bits. Avoid fries, onion rings, coleslaw, creamy salads, and buttered mashed potatoes. Also, limit yourself to one roll or slice of bread.
4. **On sandwiches,** hold the mayonnaise or special sauce and replace it with mustard, fat-free salad dressing, barbecue sauce, or horseradish. It's best to remove the cheese, but if you have to have it, request a smaller amount or order low-fat varieties when available.
5. **Ask for a to-go container** when you order your meal. When your food arrives, immediately pack up a portion to take home and set it aside.
6. **Order creatively.** It isn't essential to order an entrée when dining out. Mix and match low-fat appetizers, salads, and soups.
7. **When choosing a high-calorie menu item,** try to combine it with a light accompaniment, such as a salad with light dressing, steamed vegetables, or a broth-based soup.
8. **Steer clear of liquid calories.** Limit your beverage choices to water, diet soda, unsweetened or artificially sweetened iced tea, hot tea, or coffee. Avoid fruit juices and all other presweetened beverages to keep calories down.
9. **Be careful not to assume** that all salads are "light." The addition of high-fat toppings, such as cheese, bacon, fried tortilla strips, nuts, avocado, croutons, and oily dressings, can rack up calories and fat. Ask that these ingredients be used sparingly or served on the side.
10. **If choosing an appetizer,** stick to steamed seafood, steamed pot stickers or spring rolls, pita bread with raw vegetables and hummus, grilled chicken skewers, or broth-based soup.
11. **Eat slowly.** Dining out is often more about interacting with your fellow diners than the food itself. Take time to put your fork down and enjoy the company of friends or family.
12. **Choose desserts wisely—if at all.** Fresh fruit or a small serving of sorbet or low-fat yogurt is best. Avoid desserts with whipped cream and full-fat ice cream.

index

metric information

The charts on this page provide a guide for converting measurements from the U.S. customary system, which is used throughout this book, to the metric system.

Product Differences

Most of the ingredients called for in the recipes in this book are available in most countries. However, some are known by different names. Here are some common American ingredients and their possible counterparts:

❋ All-purpose flour is enriched, bleached or unbleached white household flour. When self-rising flour is used in place of all-purpose flour in a recipe that calls for leavening, omit the leavening agent (baking soda or baking powder) and salt.

❋ Baking soda is bicarbonate of soda.

❋ Cornstarch is cornflour.

❋ Golden raisins are sultanas.

❋ Light-colored corn syrup is golden syrup.

❋ Powdered sugar is icing sugar.

❋ Sugar (white) is granulated, fine granulated, or castor sugar.

❋ Vanilla or vanilla extract is vanilla essence.

Volume and Weight

The United States traditionally uses cup measures for liquid and solid ingredients. The chart below shows the approximate imperial and metric equivalents. If you are accustomed to weighing solid ingredients, the following approximate equivalents will be helpful.

❋ 1 cup butter, castor sugar, or rice = 8 ounces = 1/2 pound = 250 grams

❋ 1 cup flour = 4 ounces = 1/4 pound = 125 grams

❋ 1 cup icing sugar = 5 ounces = 150 grams

Canadian and U.S. volume for a cup measure is 8 fluid ounces (237 ml), but the standard metric equivalent is 250 ml.

1 British imperial cup is 10 fluid ounces.

In Australia, 1 tablespoon equals 20 ml, and there are 4 teaspoons in the Australian tablespoon.

Spoon measures are used for smaller amounts of ingredients. Although the size of the tablespoon varies slightly in different countries, for practical purposes and for recipes in this book, a straight substitution is all that's necessary. Measurements made using cups or spoons always should be level unless stated otherwise.

Common Weight Range Replacements

Imperial / U.S.	Metric
1/2 ounce	15 g
1 ounce	25 g or 30 g
4 ounces (1/4 pound)	115 g or 125 g
8 ounces (1/2 pound)	225 g or 250 g
16 ounces (1 pound)	450 g or 500 g
1 1/4 pounds	625 g
1 1/2 pounds	750 g
2 pounds or 2 1/4 pounds	1,000 g or 1 Kg

Oven Temperature Equivalents

Fahrenheit Setting	Celsius Setting*	Gas Setting
300°F	150°C	Gas Mark 2 (very low)
325°F	160°C	Gas Mark 3 (low)
350°F	180°C	Gas Mark 4 (moderate)
375°F	190°C	Gas Mark 5 (moderate)
400°F	200°C	Gas Mark 6 (hot)
425°F	220°C	Gas Mark 7 (hot)
450°F	230°C	Gas Mark 8 (very hot)
475°F	240°C	Gas Mark 9 (very hot)
500°F	260°C	Gas Mark 10 (extremely hot)
Broil	Broil	Grill

*Electric and gas ovens may be calibrated using celsius. However, for an electric oven, increase celsius setting 10 to 20 degrees when cooking above 160°C. For convection or forced air ovens (gas or electric), lower the temperature setting 25°F/10°C when cooking at all heat levels.

Baking Pan Sizes

Imperial / U.S.	Metric
9×1 1/2-inch round cake pan	22- or 23×4-cm (1.5 L)
9×1 1/2-inch pie plate	22- or 23×4-cm (1 L)
8×8×2-inch square cake pan	20×5-cm (2 L)
9×9×2-inch square cake pan	22- or 23×4.5-cm (2.5 L)
11×7×1 1/2-inch baking pan	28×17×4-cm (2 L)
2-quart rectangular baking pan	30×19×4.5-cm (3 L)
13×9×2-inch baking pan	34×22×4.5-cm (3.5 L)
15×10×1-inch jelly roll pan	40×25×2-cm
9×5×3-inch loaf pan	23×13×8-cm (2 L)
2-quart casserole	2 L

U.S. / Standard Metric Equivalents

1/8 teaspoon = 0.5 ml	
1/4 teaspoon = 1 ml	
1/2 teaspoon = 2 ml	
1 teaspoon = 5 ml	
1 tablespoon = 15 ml	
2 tablespoons = 25 ml	
1/4 cup = 2 fluid ounces = 50 ml	
1/3 cup = 3 fluid ounces = 75 ml	
1/2 cup = 4 fluid ounces = 125 ml	
2/3 cup = 5 fluid ounces = 150 ml	
3/4 cup = 6 fluid ounces = 175 ml	
1 cup = 8 fluid ounces = 250 ml	
2 cups = 1 pint = 500 ml	
1 quart = 1 litre	

DIABETIC LIVING™ series Holiday Cooking (ISBN 978-0-696-23992-2, ISSN 1557-248X), Volume 1. The DIABETIC LIVING cookbook series is published biannually by Meredith Corp., 1716 Locust St., Des Moines, IA 50309-3023. DIABETIC LIVING® magazine SUBSCRIPTION PRICES: U.S. and its possessions, 1 year $19.97; Canada and other countries, 1 year $23.97.